SOFT MONEY
HARD LAW

A GUIDE TO THE NEW CAMPAIGN FINANCE LAW

ROBERT F. BAUER

ACKNOWLEDGMENTS

I am very grateful for the assistance of a number of people who, seeing that I intended to put this book out in a short time, shrugged off their doubts and offered me their help.

My colleagues Judy Corley, Marc Elias, and Brian Svoboda were the unlucky members of the Political Law Group enlisted to read and re-read the manuscript, as it was revised, to scour it for errors and exaggerations, and to help me think through this or that issue. Donna Lovecchio provided, as she always does, first-rate research—and as always, with remarkable speed. Cindy Campos kept the production on schedule and did not complain about the obsessive daily revisions. Sheila Johnson gave up time on weekends to this enterprise, as she has given up evenings and weekends in the past to skillfully help me through my projects. I am indebted to Laurie Painter for her superb design work. And Jennifer Carney coordinated, with her usual good humor and exemplary efficiency, the development of the concept and its execution and production from beginning to end. I am indebted to the other members of the Group who carried on with their regular duties and overlooked the madness. And my wife Anita supported this project in every way, with advice but also patience.

Contents

AN INTRODUCTION

The law discussed in this book has been known in the Senate as McCain-Feingold, and in the House as Shays-Meehan, but its official "short title" is the "Bipartisan Campaign Reform Act of 2002." [1] And so it will be cited as the Act throughout this book. The law that it amends, the Federal Election Campaign Act, will be termed "existing law" and indeed it will exist generally until November 6, 2002.

What's in a name?

The Act is intended mainly as an attempt to control "soft money." This is a term with a confused history, but it refers primarily to monies spent by unions and corporations for political purposes, and also to spending by individuals beyond the relatively modest limits set by federal law. It is not a longstanding legal term of art—it did not appear in federal law until the passage of this Act.

To some extent, the term encompasses any political spending believed in some fashion inimical to sound democratic practice. An example is spending by millionaires—or more precisely, by people with a lot of money, whether in the millions or not—to advance their candidacies for federal office. The Act tries to protect candidates who do not have lots of money to spend, from opponents who do, and the way in which it proposes to do this is complex. Is spending by the wealthy "soft money?" Probably not—because while the Act attempts to limit their influence, this spending is lawful, protected indeed by the First Amendment as it has been read by the U.S. Supreme Court. By contrast, those strongly favoring the Act have generally viewed "soft money" as a loophole exploited by parties and others to navigate around legal restrictions on unions, corporations, and individual spending.

"Soft money": apparently not good

Hence the Act aims principally to control soft money spent by political parties, though it treats national parties differently—and more restrictively—than state or local

The problem with party "soft money"

---

[1] The "long title" appears to be "AN ACT To Amend the Federal Election Campaign Act of 1971 to provide bipartisan campaign reform." Difference between the long and the short: 10 words. Significance: None.

[2] Hence, in the words of a key sponsor in the Senate: "The ban on soft money defines the legislation." 147 Cong. Rec. S2886 (daily ed. Mar. 26, 2001) (statement of Sen. Feingold).

parties.[2] By and large national parties, and those associated with them, may not have anything to do with soft money—may not raise or receive, or have any direct hand in spending soft money.[3] State and local parties are allowed more leeway, particularly to raise and spend soft money where their purpose is solely to advance the prospects of state and local candidates. Yet the Act assumes that in each election where a federal candidate *appears* on the state ballot, state and local party activity has some federal election effect; and so in that case, the Act sharply restricts the soft money that state and local parties can spend for a variety of general party purposes, such as voter registration and get-out-the-vote (GOTV) activities.

The Act also addresses "soft money" spent in different ways by organizations that spend resources to influence the public's opinions on public policy issues, and also on candidates and officeholders. For purposes of this book, the term "outside groups" refers to corporations, unions, committees, or other groups, and it is used to distinguish these entities from parties, and also from political committees controlled by and contributing to candidates. Whether all organizations traveling by that name are "independent" from, say, candidates, is often hotly disputed. At any rate, these organizations also spend "soft money," and, unlike parties, that is all they spend: they raise and spend funds without regard to federal limits, and except in certain limited instances, they do not disclose to the public their resources or how they spend them.

Outside Groups' "soft money": the problem with mentioning Congressman Jones

Moreover, these groups will dispute that their ads are even intended to influence elections, insisting that they are merely seeking to express themselves on the issues of the day. Example: "Congressman Jones voted seven times to sell your children into slavery. Call Congressman Jones today, and tell him to drop dead." Now where, these organizations ask, does there appear in this sort of ad any expressed appeal to viewers or listeners to VOTE one way or the other?[4]

But, for several reasons, the Act does not go as far in restricting these outside groups as it does in the case of

---

[3] "The purpose of these provisions is simple: to put the national parties entirely out of the soft money business." 148 Cong. Rec. H408 (daily ed. Feb. 13, 2002) (statement of Rep. Shays).

political parties, and the reasons are several. First, the drafters believe that soft money contributed to parties is contributed, in effect, to their candidates, and presents the greater danger of violating the longstanding prohibition on corporate, union, and unlimited individual contributions to candidates. Second, the drafters imagined that a broad ban on soft money spending by political parties stood a better chance of surviving Supreme Court review than a ban on spending by "outside groups." Third, there are some in the Congress who, believing fervently in the constitutional rights of these kinds or organizations, would not have supported the Act if a ban on spending by "outside groups" had been more harshly treated.

The Act, while most aggressive in its treatment of soft money, does seek to limit the effects of other political spending thought unhelpful to healthy politics. In addition to its concern with spending by wealthy candidates, the bill also addresses other campaign finance issues, such as the making of contributions by minor children, the raising of contributions on federal property, and contributions by foreign nationals. It looks overall to improved enforcement by promulgating new disclosure requirements, and by assessing enhanced penalties—including most notably, new criminal penalties—for certain violations.

The Act also departs from its main theme in one key respect—by raising "hard" money contribution limits. It allows individuals to contribute twice as much to candidates as existing law permits, and it raises the limit for their contributions to state and national political parties. To make room for this additional authority, it also raises the aggregate limit on an individual's contributions to candidates and political committees. In a sense, this is a departure, as stated: the law generally limits giving, and these provisions encourage more of it. But in another sense, the increased individual limits

But up with the hard money

---

[4] As one Congressional supporter of reform has stated the case against these ads: "Today corporations, wealthy individuals, and others can spend unlimited amounts of money running political ads as long as they do not ask people to vote for or against a candidate. These phony issue ads...have become the weapon of choice..." 147 Cong. Rec. S2886 (daily ed. Mar. 26, 2001) (statement of Sen. Kennedy).

serve the tactical necessity of offering some additional resources to replace the ones, in the form of prohibited soft money, that are lost.

This book will try to lay out all of these restrictions and provisions in reasonable detail, providing where necessary background on the existing law so that the new one makes some sense. Past is prologue, it is said, and much of the Act—indeed virtually all of it—is a reaction to a perceived breakdown in the existing regulatory regime. As noted, "soft money" is believed to be an escape from controls on political money enacted beginning with the first decade of the 20th century, when Congress passed and Theodore Roosevelt signed a prohibition on corporate contributions in federal elections.[5] Those provisions of the bill concerned with "issue advertising" paid with soft money, hark back to the advent of this kind of advertising in the 1990s by parties and outside groups, and to the alleged inability of the Federal Election Commission (FEC) to deal with the problem. Other provisions tightening penalties for enforcement are intended to shore up weak regulatory enforcement, and to put the Fear of Government into political actors supposedly grown accustomed to working the fringes of the law.

Soon....the Courts and the FEC will have their say

One of the difficulties of this exposition, so soon after the effective date of the Act, is that much "law" remains to be made. The FEC will produce implementing rules. Those rules could prove of supreme importance in defining the practical effect of certain key provisions of the bill. For the most part, the FEC carries out its work in considerable anonymity, with few reporters in attendance at its public meetings and few witnesses to provide written or oral testimony on pending rulemaking issues. It remains to be seen whether this rulemaking will be any different. Then, there is the matter of litigation, which as of this printing has already been filed, launched on constitutional claims against the major pieces of the legislation. Between the litigation

---

[5] "I just point out we are trying to enforce the 1907 law banning the corporate treasury money, the 1947 law banning union dues money, and the 1974 law which bans unlimited sums by one individual in a campaign and to enforce all three laws." 148 Cong. Rec. H345 (daily ed. Feb. 13, 2002) (statement of Rep. Shays).

and the rules, much of what appears in the text of the Act as passed may undergo significant interpretative transformation, or may, by the stroke of judges' hands, disappear altogether.

So what appears in the following pages tells only the early part of the story, and it does not attempt to supply exhaustive detail, or answer every question; but its purpose is to provide a basic understanding of the structure and purpose of the law. It is, after all, only fair that those expected to comply with the law, such as candidates, parties, officeholders, contributors, and volunteers, should have multiple opportunities to understand it. As the political laws of the land become both more voluminous and more complex, the task of understanding becomes also more demanding. Consulting a lawyer can help—but it is expensive, and not always enlightening. Few care to contemplate the pleasures of politics while being billed, sometimes enthusiastically, by the hour.

So this Guide might, for some, who just wish to have an idea how all this works, raise the understanding while lowering the bill. It is meant to be user-friendly— not heavy on citations and liberal with examples. More specific questions about the Act, particularly questions about its application to proposed political activities, may in all prudence require a lawyer's attention.

A book costs less than a consultation

The use of "legislative history" in this book in exploring the meaning of various provisions of the Act requires some explanation. There was no substantial Committee report explaining the intended purpose of various provisions, and the floor debates also are bereft of detailed exposition. Of course, there are those commentators, even Justices of the U.S. Supreme Court, who are skeptical about the value or meaning of "legislative history." Nonetheless, the book refers to statements by sponsors of the Act of their "intent" behind certain important provisions. The statements may not be decisive on these points, but surely they will to some extent influence views about the issues they address. The FEC, for example, is likely to pay some attention to these statements as they develop rules implementing the Act.

CHAPTER 1

THE POLITICAL PARTIES

1. Background: The Question of Parties and Their Soft Money

The very possibility of party "soft money," in theory, arises from the varied activities of political parties in supporting candidates at all levels of government—federal, state, and local. Federal law does not permit parties to spend certain kinds of monies, such as corporate monies, to support federal candidates, but state and local laws control the monies spent to support state and local candidates. A number of states allow monies for state and local races that would be disallowed by federal law for federal races,[6] and impose different limits on contributions to candidates and parties than the ones in federal law. Parties, therefore, operate under different sets of laws for different activities, depending on where in the political process—federal, state, or local—they take place.

"Hard" money for federal candidates... "soft" for the others

As a result, relatively early in the life of the "Watergate" reforms of the 1970s, parties established different accounts for these different activities. Federal accounts held the monies needed and allowed for federal races, while nonfederal accounts held the funds that state and local laws permitted for the support of state and local candidates. The operation of these different accounts was not controversial as long as parties simply contributed monies from these accounts directly to candidates. Controversy flamed into view as parties paid for "mixed activities"—activities that by their nature affected candidates throughout the ballot. A simple example: voter registration, which results in voters who, once registered, will cast a ballot up and down the ticket for federal, as well as state and local candidates. Which monies in which accounts could be used?

---

[6] For example, 29 states authorize corporate contributions to state and local candidates. States like Texas, Pennsylvania, and Illinois allow individuals to contribute substantially more to state and local candidates than they may contribute under federal law to federal candidates.

FEC "allocation" rules

The FEC concluded that parties could pay for these expenses out of each of their accounts, in some "mix" or predetermined portion. That portion was generally determined by the composition of the ballot for a particular election, and specifically by the relative number of federal and nonfederal candidates. If federal candidates made up 25% of the number of candidates on the state ballot, then the state party would have to finance 25% of the costs of "mixed" activity, like voter registration, with federal or "hard funds" subject to federal law limits. The balance of 75% could be paid with funds held in state and local accounts—with "soft money."

Critics concluded that these "allocation rules" allowed for "soft money" to underwrite too large a share of the costs of these activities. State and local races outnumber federal ones, and so the percentage of the cost assigned to them will generally be higher—far higher—than that assigned to the federal races. Yet, the critics claimed, federal and state races should not be weighed on the same scale, that is, treated as equivalent. In their view, a race for the U.S. Senate mattered more than a race for county council, and so the decision to weight them the same in any formula simply allowed more "soft money" to seep into the parties' financing of federal races.

Court to FEC: "Not good enough"

The critics sued, as critics often do, and a court agreed that the FEC had not adequately thought through how to handle the financing of these mixed activities.[7] The FEC was ordered to produce new rules, and after some time, it did. Under these new rules, federal races and others were not weighted the same, with the result that while parties could still pay for "mixed activities" with both federal and nonfederal funds, the share paid from federal funds had to be higher than before. In addition to the assumption that federal offices counted more than others, it was assumed also that national parties, those directed at the federal level, cared less about state and local than they did about federal races. The rules established for these national parties fixed minimum percentages for the federal share of certain mixed activities—60% or 65%, depending on whether the committee was the national

---

[7] *Common Cause v. FEC*, 692 F. Supp. 1391 (D.D.C. 1987).

committee of the party or one of its Congressional campaign committees, and whether the spending occurred in a presidential or nonpresidential year. Those rules were still more complicated, requiring a different approach to the financing of different mixed activities, such as "administrative," "fundraising," and "generic" party activities.

These rules were promulgated in 1991, but they did not quiet the critics for long. By 1995, the FEC had addressed the requirements for what has come to be known as "issue advertising." This advertising by parties and others lauds or attacks a federal candidate, or an officeholder who is a candidate, for a position on an issue. These ads typically urge the viewers to call those officeholders to praise them or invite them to burn in hell. A telephone number typically, but not always, appears on the screen to facilitate the proposed contact with the named candidate-officeholder. What does not appear in the ad are "magic words" exhibiting a clear-cut intention to affect the outcome of an election—words like "vote," "defeat," "support," or "don't you wish that you would never see or hear from him again?" The FEC dutifully suggested that this could be an "administrative" expense of the party, payable on a "mixed" basis from both hard and soft money accounts.[8] Of course, only federal candidates or officeholders would generally appear in these ads, but the premise of the FEC's ruling was that the purpose of the ad was to influence opinion and action on issues, not elections.

The advent of issue advertising

The unhappy critics of the early 1990s became the reform warriors of the late 1990s. To them, this latest development demonstrated that the election laws as envisioned in 1974 had collapsed. They believed that parties, on the thinnest of excuses, were spending soft money liberally for attack ads with the clear effect and the probable intent of influencing federal campaigns. Some of these kinds of ads appeared on the air, and others in the mail; but they appeared on the wings of some millions of dollars. "Special interests"—never clearly defined but meant to include anyone organized

A world gone mad...

[8] FEC Advisory Opinion 1995-25.

and well funded for political activity—provided the funds directly to federal candidates and officeholders who collected them for the parties. The sin lay in both directions—in the raising of the money by candidates and officeholders, and in the spending of the money by the parties to help them.[9] If the existing law had prohibited corporate and labor contributions to candidates, and also unlimited individual donations, what could explain the millions in this kind of money flowing through the parties—if not a breakdown in the law?

Outside groups joined the fray, first challenging the parties for dominance of the airwaves, then receding somewhat and focusing their "soft money" initiatives on mailings and door-to-door mobilization of voters. Republicans, generally suspicious of government interference in campaign finance, developed religion on the subject as they attacked the use of party soft money in supporting President Clinton's 1996 presidential re-election campaign.[10] Democrats pointed to the same use of soft money in the same presidential election year by the Republican nominee Robert Dole, but actively supported legislative reform.

Critics demanded legislation, but they also attempted litigation. The FEC, too, was drawn into the fight by the claims and counterclaims of the parties as each protested that their issue ads were legal while the other's were not.[11] All of these battles were fought to a stalemate. Only legislation remained to address the problem.

2. National Parties, Soft Money, and the New Law

What's a national committee of a political party?

Each of the major parties operates three national organizations recognized at federal law: the national committee of each party,[12] and the "congressional campaign commit-

---

[9] David B. Magleby, ed., *Outside Money: Soft Money and Issue Advocacy in 1998 Congressional Elections* (2000).

[10] Investigation of Illegal or Improper Activities in Connection with 1996 Federal Election Campaigns, Final Report of the Comm. on Gov't Affairs, S. Rep. No. 105-167 (1998).

[11] Report of the Audit Division on Clinton/Gore '96 General Committee, Inc. and Clinton/Gore '96 General Election Legal and Accounting Compliance Fund; Report of the Audit Division on the Dole/Kemp '96 and Dole/Kemp Compliance Committee, Inc. (General).

tees" representing the parties' interests in House and Senate, as well as other elections.[13] The Act imposes different rules on the different kinds of political party committees, and national party committees take the lash more than the others.

Under the Act, these committees are broadly restricted to raising and spending only hard money—that is, monies "subject to the limitations, prohibitions, and reporting requirements of the Act." That means—

—They may <u>not</u> receive corporate or union contributions.

—They <u>may</u> accept contributions from the "multi-candidate" political committees or PACs established by corporations and unions, or other PACs, up to the applicable limits, generally, $15,000 per calendar year.[14]

—They <u>may</u> receive contributions from individuals in an amount per individual up to $25,000 per calendar year—and no more. *BUT individuals must contribute to parties within an overall limit in any two-year election cycle on all their contributions to FEC-registered political committees and federal candidates.*[15]

What they can raise.... and what they cannot

[12] In the case of the major parties, these are the Democratic and Republican National Committees.

[13] The National Republican Senatorial Committee and the Democratic Senatorial Campaign Committee, active on the Senate level, and the Democratic Congressional Campaign Committee and National Republican Congressional Committee, active in House campaigns. These committees answer to and are directed in their operations by the incumbent Members of the Senate and House of each party.

[14] As under existing law, there remains a difference under the Act between the contribution limits of "multicandidate" PACs and other non-multican-didate committees. Most corporate and union PACs are "multicandidates," which means that they have been registered with the FEC for at least 6 months, have supported at least 5 federal candidates, and received contributions from more than 50 persons. Under the new law, effective in 2003, a multicandidate PAC may contribute, as under existing law, $15,000 to a national party committee in a calendar year, while a PAC not satisfying multicandidate status may contribute $25,000. Most reasonably active PACs, likely to provide support at a the federal level, will be multicandidates and will have to comply with the $15,000 annual limit.

[15] See below for a discussion of this limit. Also note that the Act does not allow the parties to accept contributions from foreign nationals lacking permanent resident status, a much open question after the 1996 presidential elections.

The Act "indexes" these contribution limits for inflation, and so they will change to numbers calculated and published by the FEC.

Prohibiting national parties from soliciting, receiving, or directing "soft money"

National party committees may solicit and receive these monies—hard monies—but they are prohibited absolutely from soliciting, receiving, or directing any soft money "to another person." Parties do not, of course, do these things—people do—and so the Act makes clear that this prohibition falls 1) on parties' "officers" or "agents" who are "acting on their behalf," 2) federal candidates or officeholders, or 3) any "entity" that parties establish, finance, maintain, or control.

Now because parties may not spend soft money under the Act, then a fair question is why the statute bothers with a prohibition on the solicitation of such monies. Why would anyone solicit funds that cannot be received or used? The answer may lie in the additional restriction—"directing to another person" such monies. The Act has mounted the parapet and is maintaining a watch over the more indirect solicitation of "soft" funds by persons acting on behalf of the national party committee and its purposes.

A national party committee "agent" might otherwise, for example, solicit contributions for another organization able to receive them—such as a tax-exempt organization engaged in voter registration or GOTV activity. It might do so on the express understanding with the donor and the other organization that the monies would be used for these purposes. Or these "agents" could raise the money for an "independent group" buying time for "issue ads" on a major public policy issue thought helpful to that party.

Officers and "agents" of national parties

May the law successfully prevent someone active with the party from stepping outside that role and raising monies for other political purposes elsewhere, for other organizations? Here the prohibition adjusts its sights somewhat, and proposes to prohibit only those fundraising activities by officers and agents "acting on behalf" of the national committee. A vice chair of a national party may be involved with voter registration elsewhere, with other organizations that are not political parties. She appears able under the Act to raise money for them—if not doing so "on behalf" of the party. It may be clear when the vice chair is acting "on behalf" of the party, as for example, when the Chair directs him to do so, explaining in telling detail the importance to the party of the registration efforts. But the vice chair also may just know that this activity is important, and from the beginning of her public career, may have separately pursued the goal of encouraging tax exempt organizations to register voters. The Act does not say when, in performing both roles, she is carrying out her tax-exempt fundraising "on behalf of" the party.

This is a complicated enough point about the role of officers, and still another will shape the fate of those who are not officers but could be deemed to be "agents." The Act does not define "agent," but current FEC rules do, and until supplanted by any new agency rulemaking, these existing rules define the issue. An agent is one who seems to have certain authority within the party either—1) authority, express or implied, to make or authorize the making of party expenditures for any candidate, or 2) the authority derived from a position within the party "where it would reasonably appear that in the ordinary course of campaign-related activities, he or she may authorize expenditures."[16] The responsibility in question turns on the authority to "authorize expenditures." The rule does not add much detail to the point. A volunteer offering time to the party might incur reimbursable expenses for local cab fare—which is a form of "authorizing expenditures"—but this hardly seems sufficient to justify a restriction on her other political activities in raising monies for tax-exempts or issue organizations.

More on "agents"

Of course, the Act does place the restrictions more narrowly on those "agents" who are "acting on behalf of" the party. This produces more tautology than enlightenment, because an "agent" by definition is acting on behalf of the party in *some* context. "Acting on

---

[16] 11 C.F.R. § 109(b)(5) (2002).

behalf" as a phrase is seemingly meant to add something to the meaning of "agent," but its practical effect is unclear. As noted in the case of officers, a direct instruction from party to agent would prepare the ground for some action "on the party's behalf." It is unlikely that most significant issues under this Act will be presented by the most obvious actions.

Smith is the treasurer of a national party committee, and he is anxious about voting turnout in a Congressional race. In the course of a conversation with Turner, a philanthropist affiliated with the same party, he stresses the critical role of resources for turnout. He invites Turner to discuss current plans for turnout with a nonprofit community organization that devotes money and personnel to "getting out the vote."

Later a memo surfaces in the press, detailing a) the conversation, b) Turner's subsequent meeting with the community organization; and c) Turner's donation of substantial funds to the community organization to support its turnout efforts. The opposition party demands an investigation, claiming on these facts that Treasurer Smith "solicited" soft money from Turner in violation of the Act. Everybody hurriedly hires lawyers.

In the preceding example, Treasurer Smith could mount defenses under the Act that even if he did have the stated meeting with Philanthropist Turner, he did not "solicit" him. He merely commented on the need for resources to Turner, never explicitly asking Turner to contribute to the community organization. Turner, in turn, did what he thought it made sense to do. Smith also could deny that he was "acting on behalf of" the party. He did not act on formal instructions from the party: he was merely discussing the Congressional race with Turner, who has known him for years and often discussed with him the political issues of the day.

So goes Turner's defenses, but the Act has put into play questions of fact—what did he say? Was he indeed acting for himself? That could require investigation to settle. For example, the memo that came to light would not be helpful to Turner's case, if he had prepared it on national party committee stationery, addressed it to the chairman of the party, and concluded with the words: "We should consider enlisting Turner's support again in the future, in other races where money for turnout would be critical to our chances for success." The investigating agency would find this memo damning on the question of whether he was acting in his official capacity, and also whether he had intended to "solicit" Turner for money to the community group.

The provision in question also seeks to head off any effort of a national party committee to establish some other organization, or finance or control one, to solicit or direct soft money for its political purposes. The national committees cannot, for example, establish their own local community organizations, dedicated to nonpartisan voter turnout, which would propose to accept soft money.

Another provision more specifically bars the national parties—and as noted below, also state and local committees—from soliciting funds for, or financially supporting, either 1) 501(c) tax-exempt organizations engaged in activities "in connection with" federal elections, such as voter registration or GOTV activities, or 2) so-called "527" organizations.

Prohibiting solicitations of certain tax-exempts and 527s

At this point, some explanation is needed for the term "527" organization. These are organizations treated under the tax laws as political committees, which means that they are not required to pay tax on the contributions they raise for their election-related activity. A 527 organization may elect not to contribute monies to, or coordinate its activities with, federal candidates; and so it may not be a "political committee" compelled to register with the FEC and comply with limits on the source and amounts of contributions. In other words, these types of organizations may take "soft money"—indeed any kind of money from anyone in any amount. 527s of this kind register with and report their activities to the Internal Revenue Service only, not the FEC. Their activities might consist of educating voters on issues, or conducting voter registration and GOTV activity.[17]

What is a "527"?

Under the Act, national parties may not raise monies for these 527s, nor for other kinds of tax-exempts, like

501(c)(3) charitable organizations or 501(c)(4) "social welfare" organizations, on the theory that these other organizations could serve as vehicles for the parties to avoid their own soft money limits. This prohibition does not depend on whether these tax-exempt organizations are nonpartisan or partisan, or whether the national committee in raising the money directs how it is spent. The prohibition is absolute: the parties may not assist these organizations with soft money fundraising.

The national committee of a political party is impressed with a tax-exempt organization committed to educating voters on the right to vote, and recruiting "first-time" voters in disadvantaged communities. The national committee has never coordinated its activities with the group, because the group seeks to maintain its reputation as nonpartisan. The Chair of the Committee, speaking to a meeting of party activists and donors, notes the organization's work, closing with the remark: "This is important work, and all of us in the party should support it. Give it your time, or give it your money—but please do what you can." The Chair has violated the Act's prohibition on "soliciting" funds for tax-exempts engaged in this kind of work.

Watching what officers and agents of parties say— not just what they do

As will be noted below in other contexts, a large part of the stringency of these provisions—and their difficulty—is their focus on "soliciting" and "directing." Soliciting and directing can involve actions, but they also can take place in the course of ordinary political communication. Existing law contains some limited prohibitions aimed at other kinds of "solicitations": it does not permit, for example, a corporation or union to solicit contributions from the general public. (Corporations may solicit management, employees, and shareholders, while unions may solicit their members). The national party provisions repre-

---

[17] For a useful and more detailed discussion of "527"s, within the overall context of changes in the world of campaign finance, see Frances R. Hill, Exempt Organizations and Campaign Finance, 91 Tax Notes 477 (2001). *See also*, Richard Kornylak, "Note: Disclosing the Election-Related Activities of Interest Groups Through 527 of the Tax Code," 87 Cornell L. Rev. 230 (2001).

sent a considerably broader restriction on solicitations, one that falls on a political party organizations and those associated with it in the ordinary course of marshalling support for their political objectives. It compels them to watch what they say, not just what they do.

Restrictions on federal candidates and officeholders

Another—and highly significant—restriction on national party fundraising falls on federal candidates and officeholders. These are the individuals who bear the principal burden of raising money for the parties, national, as well as state and local.[18] They are "agents" of their parties for this purpose. The Act does not restrict their activities only under the "agency" rules previously described, but prohibits them as special cases from involvement with "soft money" fundraising. This prohibition states that—

> A candidate, individual holding federal office, agent of a candidate, or an individual holding federal office....shall not-
> (A) solicit, receive, direct, transfer, or spend funds in connection with an election for federal office, including funds for any federal election activity, unless the funds are subject to the limitations, prohibitions, and reporting requirements of this Act....

The Chair of the Republican National Committee (RNC) is asked by a state party for assistance in raising "soft money" for GOTV. The Chair, an officer of the RNC, cannot solicit or "direct" soft money to another. So he passes on the request to a Member of Congress from that state. The Member of Congress, however, is separately enjoined under the Act from "soft money" fundraising and cannot act in place of a party officer for this purpose.

---

[18] The Congressional campaign committees are directed by federal officeholders who join with federal candidates to raise money for the parties' congressional campaign and other political efforts.

The same Member of Congress is approached at a party event by a supporter eager to help the national party who offers to contribute $100,000 to support its activities. The Member notes that the party cannot accept a contribution of that size under the Act—it is "soft money." When the donor suggests that he would like to do more to fulfill his political objectives than the party's contribution limits allow, the Member suggests that he consider donating the money to a 527 organization, Committee for Clean Air, known to be preparing a nationwide voter education campaign on the environment. The Member, who was not asked for this assistance by the Committee, nonetheless could be liable under the Act for "directing" soft money to a 527 organization.

But candidates and officeholders can attend and speak at state party events...

Federal candidates and officeholders may, however, raise money in other capacities, and the Act makes complicated allowance for them. Federal candidates and officeholders may "attend, speak, or be a featured guest at a fundraising event for a state, district, or local committee of a political party." As will be discussed below, the state and local parties are not prohibited from raising soft money under the bill, but they are restricted in how these funds are used. Federal candidates and officeholders may help with this soft money fundraising as attendees, featured guests, or speakers.

A federal officeholder is invited to participate as the featured guest and to speak at a fundraising event for a county committee of his party. He is asked to exhort those in attendance to "give what you can" to the county committee to support its various political programs. Although he is clearly soliciting "soft money," which the county committee may accept for various purposes, he may accept the invitation under the exception for attending and speaking at a state or local party fundraising event.

After the event, the officeholder is invited to a private reception for the county committee's most honored guests, including its largest contributors. The Chairman of the local committee requests that he buttonhole some of these donors and press the case for large contributions. The officeholder is unsure whether he can agree to the request—the "fundraising event" at which he spoke has ended, and now he is being asked to have one-on-one conversations that could be construed under the Act to be prohibited solicitations.

May the national party refer federal candidates and officeholders to state parties for these appearances, urging the state and local parties to invite them to attend in these defined ways? The Act does not say.

The Chair of a party Senatorial campaign committee wishes to assist a state party with the raising of soft money for its various activities for which these funds can be spent. He contacts the state party Chair and offers to help arrange for an appearance at its fundraising event of a prominent U.S. Senator or Congressman. The Senatorial committee Chair is not raising money but arranging for an appearance that the Act allows, though it will result in the raising by the state party of "soft money."

While federal candidates may not raise "soft money" for party voter registration and GOTV programs, federal candidates and officeholders may do so for 501(c) educational charities engaged in these activities. A number of conditions and requirements apply, resulting in significant limitations on the kind of "charitable" fundraising related to a federal election, that these candidates and officeholders may do. The Act distinguishes between two kinds of charity—those whose principal purpose is to engage in these election-related activities and those who may conduct such activities but not as their "principal purpose."

Different rules when soliciting for charities

Charities *without* a principal purpose of funding registration and GOTV activities. Candidates and officeholders may raise funds without limit for these kinds of organizations, so long as they make only a "general solicitation" of the money and do not "specify how the funds will or should be spent." If the solicitation is specific, then only individual contributions to the charity may be solicited, and only in amounts of $20,000 per individual per calendar year.

A federal candidate chooses to raise money for the Red Cross, and she directs solicitations to a wide range of potential donors, looking for as large a contribution as any one donor can provide. The Act does not restrict this activity.

The same candidate raises money for the NAACP, which conducts a wide range of activities, including, but not as one of its "principal purposes," voter registration. The candidate may conduct a solicitation without limit on the amount raised from each donor, so long as the candidate does not suggest the monies raised will or should be spent for voter registration. If the candidate does make a statement to that effect, then the solicitation must be limited—to individuals, and to an amount requested from each individual not to exceed $20,000 per calendar year.

Charities *with* a principal purpose of funding registration and GOTV activities. Federal candidates and officeholders may raise money for charities with this principal purpose. But if they do, the Act limits the scope of the solicitation and the amount that may be solicited. The candidates or officeholders may solicit donations in these circumstances only from individuals, and then only in amounts from each donor up to $20,000 per calendar year.

What happens if a federal officeholder solicits the individuals, and seeks only $20,000 contributions, but the individual makes a contribution in a larger amount? It does not seem that the officeholder is properly held liable in this circumstance: the prohibition applies to "solicitation," and the officeholder's solicitation conformed to the limitations of the Act. It is also true, however, that the question of what was solicited is a question of fact; and if the contributor, following a conversation with an officeholder, contributes more than $20,000 to the charity, a question about the understanding between the two could be raised. For this reason, as federal candidates and officeholders consider the additional liability they face under these new solicitation restrictions, they may prudently confirm all solicitations in writing.

The national parties may encourage their federal candidates and officeholders to engage in these activities. Nothing in the Act suggests, much less states clearly, that these exceptions do not apply because of the involvement of a national party committee. Hence:

The national party requests that federal officeholders affiliated with the party assist with a major national fundraising campaign to raise charitable funds for GOTV and voter registration in minority areas. The officeholders may do so, if they comply with the requirements stated previously. They also may do so at the request of candidates who would benefit from these activities, and of the charities engaged in the registration and GOTV work.

So far the discussion has centered on the Act's restrictions on federal candidates and officeholders raising money for the national and state parties, or for functions of the national and state parties such as voter registration and GOTV activity. There are still other restrictions that apply to fundraising by candidates and officeholders for other kinds of political committees, and for state and local candidates. They are discussed in Chapter 4 ("Restrictions on Federal Candidates and Officeholders").

"Building Funds"

The existing law very directly authorized one other use of soft money by political parties—to purchase or construct an "office facility." The national parties have raised soft money to put up buildings and other related office facilities, and their soft money has paid the costs of the outstanding mortgages and other related expenses payable under the exemption. The Act ends all that, deleting the allowance effective November 6, 2002. State parties are subject to different rules in the operation of building funds, discussed further in the text below.

3. The State Parties and their "Federal Election Activity"

National parties, it has been stressed, are prohibited under the Act from raising and spending soft money. The question so far has been whether officers and agents of the parties, and the candidates who raise their funds and direct their activities, may raise soft money beneficial to party purposes without impermissibly "acting on behalf" of the party in doing so.

State and local parties are not prohibited from raising soft money in the same way. Their officers and agents are free to raise soft money, though federal candidates and officeholders—prohibited from soliciting soft money for national party committees—also are enjoined (with exceptions noted in the chapter on Restrictions on Federal Candidates and Officeholders) from such fundraising for state and local parties as well.

No Soft Money for "Federal Election Activity"

The state and local parties may not, however, "expend" or "disburse" soft money for any "federal election activity." This is the key term of the restriction, and unlike other terms used in the Act, it is specifically defined to include some activities and to exclude others. It is important to note in particular that federal election activities are not necessarily activities *intended* to influence federal elections in whole or in part. The drafters assumed that some activities conducted by parties have the *effect* of influencing federal elections, and they concluded that the effect alone justified a prohibition on the use in those activities of any monies other than the "hard money" authorized by federal law for federal elections.

"Voter registration activity" (within 120 days of an election)

The Act treats as a federal election activity "voter registration activity." It does not say more about what comprises voter registration "activity," but the regulators may conclude from the use of the term "activity" that any expenses, direct or indirect, paid to plan for, encourage, and achieve registration is "voter registration activity." The Act prohibits the use of soft money for this purpose within 120 days of the date of a regularly scheduled federal election. At all other times, the state parties may pay for these activities under the "alloca-tion" allowed under existing rules from both hard and soft funds.

A local committee launches a door-to-door registration drive in September of an election year, which will involve the election of federal as well as other candidates. All the costs associated with this registration effort—the cost of personnel, materials, phones, and print advertising— would have to be paid under the Act with hard money. Assuming that the election is taking place on November 5th, the registration drive would have to be conducted on an all-hard basis for the period of 120 days beforehand, beginning with July 5th of that year.

The Act poses for local committees, in particular, a dilemma. Any number of them may have a local focus, yielding to their State Committee's principal interest in federal races. The existing law recognizes this local emphasis, by permitting such committees to engage in a limited amount of federal election-related activities without registering as a "political committee" under federal law and becoming subject to federally imposed legal obligations.[19] By federalizing the financing of certain local party activities, such as voter registration and GOTV activities, the Act raises the likelihood that these committees will spend the level of hard money required to trigger the application to their activities of federal registration and other requirements. Whether this possibility discourages local committees from engaging at all in some of these activities remains to be seen.

"Voter identification" also qualifies under the Act as a federal election activity. Parties using phones, mail, or volunteers to identify affiliated or sympathetic voters must pay the related costs with hard money. The require-ment is not, like the one governing voter registration, pegged to a time period. Instead it applies whenever such activity is "conducted in connection with an election in which a candidate for federal office appears on the ballot."

"vote identification"...

---

[19] Other committees are subject to registration as "political committees" when spending $1,000 to influence federal elections. 2 U.S.C. § 434(4)(A).

The wording suggests that the key to the provision's application is the effect of the activity, not the timing or the intent. Voter identification by and large will affect all the candidates appearing on a party's ballot—federal and others—for the simple reason that voters once identified and exhorted to vote will have a chance to pull the lever for federal, as well as other candidates. Thus, it seems that the requirement that these activities be paid on an "all-hard" basis would apply broadly. Some states conduct nonfederal elections in years when no federal candidate appears on the ballot, and state and local parties in these states would reasonably argue that voter identification conducted in these circumstances could be paid for under existing law, with a "mix" of hard and soft money. But, of course, it also is true that the same voter identified in the off-year, for state and local elections, will be available for registration, GOTV, and advocacy in the next election cycle when federal candidates do appear again on the ballot. Are these "off-year" state and local identification efforts also being "conducted in connection with an election in which a candidate for federal office appears on the ballot"? The Act is not clear on this question.

"Get-out-the-vote and party promotional activities"...

GOVT activity—the business of actually motivating voters and in some cases transporting them to the polls—also is a federal election activity, and the requirement of "all-hard" financing applies also to any of these activities conducted "in connection with" a federal election. "All hard" financing also is required for "generic campaign activity," which is defined as "a campaign activity that promotes a political party and does not promote a candidate or non-federal candidate." The two activities, GOTV and generic campaign activity, may be closely related in function, as in the case of appeals to the public to "Vote Democratic," or "Vote Republican." This relationship is not fixed, however, and a party also may advertise its virtues at some distance from an election to solidify party identification and for other political purposes.

A state party committee funds door hangers with an appeal to voters to "get out and cast your ballot for the Confused Party on Election Day. Vote Confused!" If the activity is conducted in a year when federal candidates appear on the ballot, the Act requires that the attributable costs be paid with hard money only.

Then there is the matter of "issue advertising," described earlier as one of the controversial practices fueling support for the Act. The Act does not make specific mention of "issue advertising," but it does include within the term "federal election activity," any

"Issues advertising"

> [P]ublic communication that refers to a clearly identified candidate for federal office (regardless of whether a candidate for state or local office is also mentioned or identified) and that promotes or supports a candidate for that office, or attacks or opposes a candidate for that office (regardless of whether the communication expressly advocates a vote for or against a candidate).

The public communication described in this communication need not include "express advocacy"—the magic words that include "vote," "reject," "defeat," or the like. The provision turns instead on one objective factor, and another factor that is altogether subjective in nature.

The public communication must, in a relatively objective sense, "refer" to a clearly identified candidate. The term "clearly identified" appears in existing law, and it encompasses the name of the candidate, a drawing or photograph, or some way in which her identity "is apparent by unambiguous reference." [20] More subjectively, the public communication also must then "promote or support," or alternatively "attack or oppose," that candidate. The typical issue ad is rarely reticent in the expression of its views about a candidate. The reader is familiar with the standard approach—a grainy image, with a blurred black and white of the candidate, and a litany of appalling acts with which she is charged, followed by "Call Marcia Jones. Tell her that public office is a public trust, not a chance for her and her friends to feed at the trough." [21]

---

[20] 2 U.S.C. § 431(18).

[21] Close to image of hog snorting with satisfaction over breakfast.

The Party, six months later and still Confused, runs ads intended to shore up the position of an incumbent Governor struggling with a legislature controlled by another party and contesting his leadership on a key public policy issue. The ads state that "The Confused Party is protecting your jobs and revitalizing the economy of this state. But the Simplistic Party, listening only to campaign contributions, refuses to enact desperately needed legislation to fund a true jobs program. Think about your future, then call Simplistic Party leaders and tell them—we want our government to help the people, not the special interests." Party lawyers argue over the question of whether the phrase "Simplistic Party leaders," a number of whom are federal officeholders running for reelection, "refers" to "clearly identified candidates," and therefore bars the use of soft money to pay for the ad.

The Confused Party decides to run the ad featuring a key supporter of the Governor, the senior U.S. Senator of the State who also is running for reelection. He appears on-camera to speak warmly of the Governor's leadership, and the Governor closes the ad, declaring that "I am proud of the help that Senator Smiles and I have been privileged to provide to the working families of this state." Opponents of the Governor and Senator Smiles file a complaint, alleging that the Party had financed with soft money a public communication, inasmuch as the closing remarks of the Governor are fairly taken as promotion or support of Senator Smiles.

"Public communication" includes any "public political advertising"

The term "public communication" is very inclusive, applying to "any" form of "general" public political advertising, including "broadcast, cable, or satellite communication, newspaper, magazine, outdoor advertising facility, mass mailing, or telephone bank to the general public." A mass mailing is a mailing of more that 500 pieces of mail "of an identical or substantially similar nature within any 30-day period," while a "telephone bank" is defined in similar terms involving more than 500 calls within the same 30 day time frame.

Likely issues taken with "issue advertising"

It is likely that in the coming litigation over this bill, some complaint will be raised about the scope of this provision. Issue ads might be run throughout a cycle, well before an election and even the year before. In some cases, the party may well have as a primary purpose the pressuring of officeholders who will vote on an issue of broad public interest. While it is true that the provision applies only to public communications that "refer to a clearly identified candidate," it does not require that they be identified as a candidate. The mere fact that an officeholder also is a candidate, is enough to bring the attacks on the officeholders (or in some cases, the praise of the officeholder), within the financing restrictions of the Act.

Yet most federal officeholders are, in a technical legal sense, "candidates" throughout their term of office. The existing law requires any person who has raised and spent more than $5,000 on a campaign to file a Statement of Candidacy with the FEC or Secretary of the Senate; and most incumbent officeholders raise well beyond this amount within a short period after their most recent election and in anticipation of their next. So for federal officeholders, there is little space between their status as officeholders and their legal position as candidates.

As a result, ads critical of their official actions, even ads with little clear-cut connection to their candidacies, must be paid under the restrictive "all-hard" rule. This restriction applies to ads run the year before an election—or in the case of a Senator, several years before an election—as well as the year of an election. It also applies to ads run against candidates unlikely to draw a strong opponent, or even any. By its terms, the provision makes no distinctions on content, which means that the ads replete with scurrilous personal attacks are treated no differently from the ads offering a more reasonable critique of the officeholder's position. For these reasons, the Act stands to be questioned as overshooting the mark, limiting both campaign-related speech and other, everyday public communications on public policy issues and officeholder performance.[22]

---

[22] One of the national parties, the Republican National Committee, is maintaining as of this date a legal action under existing law directed substantially to this point. The Committee is contesting existing regulatory restrictions on issue advertising by parties which, because they do not also limit independent group issue advertising, places discriminatory speech burdens on parties. *RNC v. FEC*, No. 98-1207 (D.D.C. filed June 25, 1998).

One additional ground of complaint will become apparent in the next chapter of "electioneering communications" by outside organizations. Like parties, these organizations also are subject to a prohibition on certain kinds of "issue advertising." Unlike the party issue advertising restrictions, those imposed on "outside groups" apply only to broadcast, cablecast, or satellite communications within 30 days of a primary and 60 days of a general election. Thus, these groups can run these ads freely at all other times; and they can, at all times, finance issue advertising in the mail or through telephone banking—in all media other than radio, television, or cable.

Powerful Corporation, enraged over the energy votes of Senator Smith, finances a slew of issue ads attacking him for his votes. The ads are run up to the 30th day period prior to his primary, and then up to the 60th day before the general election. Powerful also generates glossy, well-financed mail pieces intended to bring their criticism home, which are mailed out to the Senator's constituents within these 30 and 60 day periods. Powerful spends unlimited funds from its treasury coffers for these ads.

Senator Smith complains to his state party, and demands help in responding to these attacks. The Party develops an ad defending Senator Smith's record, citing his lifelong commitment to plentiful energy resources. The Party may not use soft money for these responses, but instead must pay only with "hard money." This "all-hard" requirement applies to all of its defenses of Senator Smith directed to the general public, whether by mail, broadcast media, or other means.

As will be noted below, the problems facing the state party in funding the defense of Senator Smith are not limited to the unavailability of soft money. The Act places limits on the amount of "hard money" for this purpose, by requiring that any expenditures of the party coordinated with Smith be treated as "contributions" to Smith's campaign. As "contributions," the spending is subject to dollar limits.

The Act also defines as "federal election activity," the monthly services of a state, district, or local party committee employee who spends more than 25% of his "compensated" time in that month "on activities in connection with a federal election." In other words, should an employee in any month exceed the 25% threshold for time spent on federal election-related activities, her entire salary for the month should be paid for with hard money. The Act does not focus on activities that fall within the term federal election activity, such as voter registration or issue advertising, but any activities by that employee conducted "in connection with a federal election." This "in connection" with formulation is not defined, and leaves the parties with an open question about the application of this provision. It can be expected that the FEC will feel compelled, or will be called on, to offer some guidance on this issue through rulemaking.

Keeping an eye on the help

Exception: The Levin Amendment

The Act also identifies specific activities of state, district, and local committees that are not "federal election activity," and may be paid with a "mix" of hard and soft funds under existing law. These are not simple exclusions; they are hedged in some cases with significant qualifications. The devil lurks in the details, or more to the point, the regulators do.

Of particular importance is an exception for certain federal election activities conducted by state, district, and local party committees under certain specified conditions. This exception was added to the bill in the Senate by amendment sponsored by Senator Carl Levin of Michigan— hence, the short name, also used here, of "The Levin Amendment." [23] Its purpose was to allow for some voter registration, GOTV, voter identification, and generic party activities that could be paid on a "mixed" or "allocated" basis with hard and soft funds. The Levin amendment operates as an exception to the general rule that federal election activities must be paid on an all-hard basis.

The Levin amendment: some soft money and some federal election activity

---

[23] Changes to the amendment were made following passage by the Senate, and prior to its consideration by the House, when it was incorporated into the House version of the Act known as Shays-Meehan.

But "some restrictions apply" The amendment's application is governed by certain conditions, which are designed to allow for soft money financing of these activities without inviting much of the abuses of greatest concern to the drafters of the bill. Some of these conditions relate to the content of the activity, and others to the way the activity is conducted and financed.

Don't mention the federal candidate An activity funded under the Levin amendment may not "refer to a clearly identified candidate for federal office." Thus, a voter registration appeal funded under the conditions of the amendment may urge "Vote Democratic," but it may not frame the appeal with a reference to a candidate, such as a candidate named Jones, as follows:

When you vote this November 5th, think about the jobs created by Jones' plan—and Vote Democratic.

Or, stated differently, the Levin amendment allows for some soft financing of these kinds of appeals when a federal candidate appears on the ballot—but not when that candidate, or any other federal candidate, is named.

Stay off the air The Levin amendment also excludes from its allowances activities conducted through "broadcasting, cable, or satellite communication." Voter registration activities, for example, may under this amendment be paid with soft and hard money, including within 120 days of an federal election, but only where these activities are conducted door-to-door, by mail, or by phone. The use of radio, TV or cable to broadcast these appeals falls outside the exception. It is stressed that the party is not required to choose between one or the other means in conducting, for example, these voter registration or GOTV activities. It may fund under Levin the non-broadcast efforts with both hard and soft money, while paying on an "all-hard" basis the portion of the effort carried out through broadcast or cablecast facilities.

Limits on contributions for Levin amendment activities Restrictions on the financing of these activities are included among the conditions of the amendment. The amendment, as noted, allows for the use of both hard and soft monies for the federal election activity conducted under its conditions. The soft monies paid for this purpose must comply with the requirements of state law, which means that a state or local party may only raise for Levin amendment purposes monies that it could otherwise lawfully raise under state law for state and local elections. Moreover, the party may not raise from any one 'person' more than $10,000 in a calendar year for use in financing Levin amendment activities. This limitation is among the more unusual features of the Act, without any precedent in existing law, and deserves close attention.

Because state law controls in the first instance, this $10,000 limitation is a supplementary restriction added by the Act, but it does not supplant the state law rules. If a state's laws do not allow for corporate contributions to parties, then the Levin amendment does not supercede the state restriction.[24] A party in a state that allows the contribution of corporate contributions may raise them for Levin amendment activities, whereas a party operating in a state prohibiting corporate contributions is plumb out of luck. As another example, if state law limits contributions to a party to a level below $10,000, then this lower limit—not the $10,000 limit established by the Act—applies to a contribution made for Levin amendment purposes. So, while existing law defines "person" broadly, to include corporations, unions, individuals, and partnerships, the availability of contributions from such persons for Levin amendment activities depends on state law. State law determines who may be treated as a "person" who may contribute, and also how much they contribute.

Enforcing the limit on contributions to Levin amendment activities

The amendment also limits the "persons" who may contribute in another way, by applying the limit collectively to that "person" and any other person "established, financed, maintained, or controlled by such person." The clearest example is a corporation and its parent, subsidiaries, or affiliates. In a state where corporations may otherwise contribute to state parties under state law, the entire family of related corporations may contribute only one $10,000 contribution to a national, district, or local committee for Levin amendment activities.

---

[24] "Obviously, if a state prohibits corporate or labor union contributions to political parties, the Levin amendment does not supercede that prohibition, and corporate or union contributions of Levin money would be banned." 148 Cong. Rec. H409 (daily ed. Feb. 13, 2002) (statement of Rep. Shays).

At the same time the eligible contributor under the amendment may make a contribution to each unit of a state party—the state committee, and any of the subordinate committees of the party at the local, municipal, or district levels. The practical effect of this allowance may be limited. The reason being is it would likely be deemed inconsistent with the Act for a local committee to accept such a contribution, and to then transfer it to the state party for use in funding the actual voter registration, GOTV, or similar federal election activities. The unit of the party committee accepting the funds must make direct use of it for the specified Levin amendment activities.

There is nothing in the Act, however, to prohibit the different units of the party from collaboratively committing the monies raised under the Levin amendment to commonly conduct voter registration, GOTV, or other eligible activity. The sponsors of the bill stressed their intention that parties may not "create their own multiple subsidiary committees to raise separate $10,000 contributions under this provision."[25]

Five different county committees raise $10,000 from the same Corporation X for Levin amendment purposes— a GOTV drive conducted under the conditions of the amendment. The committees may not transfer the funds from one to the other, but they could pool their resources and coordinate their direct expenditures of these funds in the implementation of a statewide GOTV drive.

Restrictions on fundraising under the Levin amendment

Collaborative spending under the Levin amendment appears permissible, but fundraising support from other parties or from candidates is not. One additional condition of the amendment seeks to limit state and local parties to their own fundraising. As has been noted, the amendment allows for "mixed" financing of these activities with both hard and soft money. The restrictions on raising this money extend to both the hard and soft money raised for this purpose. State and local parties, and also national party committees (and their officers or agents acting on their behalf), may not provide a state or local party committee even with

---

[25] 148 Cong. Rec. H410 (daily ed. Feb. 13, 2002) (statement of Rep. Shays).

"hard" funds for Levin amendment purposes.[26] Those same committees may not establish joint fundraising ventures under which state and local parties raise hard money for their Levin amendment purposes, while the other participants raise funds for other projects and purposes. Moreover, the Act prohibits the use by state parties for Levin amendment purposes of funds provided by "any entity directly or indirectly established, financed, maintained, or controlled" by any national, state, or local committee."

Additional restrictions apply to the raising of Levin amendment "soft" monies by state and local committees. National party committees—and once again, the officers and agents acting on their behalf—may not have any part in raising soft money for parties using them for Levin amendment activities. The same restriction applies to federal candidates and officeholders. The Act will not allow any of these named committees or individuals to "solicit," "receive," "direct," or "transfer" soft funds to the state and local parties for these purposes. In fact, the Act takes the additional step of prohibiting fundraising for the parties under the Levin amendment "in the name of" national party committees, candidates or officeholders.

Levin amendment: no help from federal candidates or officeholders, or the national parties, to raise the funds

The Chair of the national Confused party is asked by the state party to call major donors of the party, explain the Levin amendment to them, and then solicit contributions directly to the state party for that purpose. The Chair of the national party may not agree to this request—or act on it. He also may not refer the request to the members of that state's congressional delegation with the intention that they would conduct this solicitation.

A friendly donor, interested in the state party's efforts, discusses the operation of the Levin amendment with a U.S. Senator from that state, and then on her own initiative, contributes $10,000 to the party under her own name with a note: "Senator Jones advises me that your

---

[26] "Furthermore, [a county committee] must itself raise the hard money allocation required by the FEC...." 148 Cong. Rec. H410 (daily ed. Feb. 13, 2002) (statement of Rep. Shays).

party could use these monies for the upcoming voter registration drive, and I am pleased to enclose a contribution for $10,000. Please make sure to credit the Senator internally for his efforts to bring this opportunity to my attention." Is this a prohibited contribution "in the name" of the officeholder? It is unclear whether it is that—or a prohibited "solicitation" by the officeholder.

State and local parties also may not collaborate in jointly raising their <u>soft</u> monies for Levin amendment activities. They may not establish joint fundraising committees for this purpose, and a state or local party committee also may not solicit such funds for the Levin amendment activities of other state and local committees. These restrictions aim to enforce a "grassroots" or local character for the activities funded under the Levin amendment. The Act's drafters appeared to believe that only "soft money" raised locally, for these state and local activities, avoids the danger of serving national or federal electoral purposes. While this concern is perhaps understandable where federal candidates, officeholders, or national committees propose to raise these funds, it is may be less clear how the perceived danger is presented by state and local committees jointly raising these monies.

Other exceptions

Exception for public communications by state and local candidates

Apart from the Levin amendment, there are other exceptions to the broad prohibition on soft money for state party "federal election activity." One applies to any "public communication" that "refers solely to a clearly identified candidate for state or local office." There is here a BUT. Even if the communication refers "solely" to such a candidate, it may not qualify for the exclusion if the communication is a voter registration, voter identification, GOTV, or generic campaign activity that would otherwise be treated as a "federal election activity." The law here has giveth, then immediately taketh away.

A state party advertises in a federal election year on behalf of a gubernatorial candidate, declaring in the ad devoted solely to that candidate that "Governor Wilson has made a difference for this state, battling the special interests and providing for more jobs to bring our economy to life. Call Governor Wilson—tell him to keep fighting for the people of this State."

So far so good—the exclusion of the Act applies, allowing the state party to fund this advertisement under the requirements and allowances of state laws. But then the Party could modify the ad and take an additional step that negates the exclusion and bring the "all hard" financing rule into play.

"We need Governor Wilson's commitment to our state's workers and families. So don't forget to vote November 5th for your family's future."

By adding the appeal to vote, in a year when a federal candidate appears on the ballot, the party has slipped away from the exception, that would have allowed for soft money financing under state law, and placed itself squarely within the all-hard financing requirement. This same result would follow if the plaudits for Governor Wilson were joined to a registration appeal, or to a broad statement in support of the party with which she was affiliated.

It is noted that the various restrictions on the financing of federal election activity apply "regardless of whether a candidate for state or local office also appears on the ballot." For example, a public communication or issue ad does not escape the Act's "all-hard" requirement simply because the advertisement discusses all senior officials of the state, including those who hold state, not federal, office.

"We need the leaders of the Simplistic Party to support a jobs program for our state's families. Call Governor Wilson and the elected leaders of our state and tell them— the time has come for the state to work for its workers."

The reference to the "elected leaders" of our state could spoil the fun for a party interested in operating within the exceptions to the all-hard financing requirements. An exclusive reference to Governor Wilson would allow the party to operate within the exception and pay with the funds allowed for these purposes under state law. But the broad reference to elected officials, including federal officeholders who also are likely candidates, may trigger the all-hard financing requirement. The ad may have become a "public communication that "refers to a clearly identified candidate for federal office (regardless of whether a candidate for state or local office is also mentioned or identified)." ("May have become," because there is perhaps some question of whether the reference to "elected officials" is a reference to "clearly identified candidates," and the ad's wording may or may not rise to the level of an ad promoting, supporting, attacking or opposing a candidate.)

Exception: contributions to state and local candidates

The complications of the exclusions also are apparent in the exception made for "a contribution to a candidate for state or local office." A party may make a soft money contribution to such a candidate, and nothing would seem more strictly nonfederal in character. The Act cautions that if the party asks that the money be spent for any of the activities defined to be "federal election activities," then this "designation" means—well, something, though it is not clear what. That the contribution cannot be made at all? That it could be made but only with "hard money"? Or with hard money and under federal contribution limits? The Act does not say.

A state party makes a soft money contribution to various state legislative candidates, but requests that each such candidate commit to the expenditure of a portion of these funds for party voter registration. If the state legislative races occur in a year in which federal candidates also appear on the ballot, the contribution has been "designated" for a federal election activity—voter registration—and the exception under the Act for this contribution does not apply.

Exception: conventions

Parties appear able under this exception to pay with mixed hard and soft funds for "the costs of a state, district, or local political convention." Because there is no qualification placed on this allowance, the party might somehow use publicity for the convention to plump for the party as a whole—to engage in some "generic" party advocacy, promoting a political party but not specific federal or other candidates. How far it might go in doing so may be tested in time; or parties may conclude that a convention is a convention, and that they may be unable to make more of them than that.

Another exclusion appears in the Act for the "costs of campaign materials," including but not limited to buttons, bumper stickers, and yard signs, but there is here, too, a BUT. Those materials may only name or depict a candidate for state and local office, and if they do, the parties may pay for them under state law, on an "all-soft" basis. This simple allowance may produce different results in different circumstances. If the materials refer to both federal and state candidates, then it would seem that the existing rules apply to allow for a "mix" of hard and soft money. If, however, the materials are produced for <u>use</u> in an activity that is treated under the Act as a federal election activity—such as a GOTV—then this expense must be included among the costs, payable solely with hard money, of that federal election activity.

Exception: campaign materials

A final allowance of note pertains to "building funds." While national party committees may not under the Act raise "soft monies" to construct or purchase office buildings, Congress elected to leave state and local parties free to do so. The monies they raise for this purpose, however, must satisfy the requirements of state law. So if state law permits a party to collect corporate contributions for an office building, the party may raise such funds for this purpose under the Act. This is a major change in the law on this point. Under existing law, federal law controlled the question of what kind of money could be used for these building projects. Now the Act abandons the field, leaving the decision on the source of funding to the various states.

Exception: building funds for state and local parties

The Act also extends the right to fund these building projects to local as well as state parties. By denying national parties the right to accept soft money for these projects, while providing for local parties to do so under state law, the Act takes the law on this point in divergent directions. The large national parties are limited in the funds available for their capital infrastructure, while much smaller local parties, with limited fields of operation, may, in many states, fund that infrastructure freely.

4. Other Limitations on Political Parties

The Act is concerned with other activities of political parties, not only their soft money issue advertising. The restrictions imposed on these activities are generally intended to keep parties from operating as vehicles for circumvention of legal limits on contributions or other expenditures to influence elections. The various kinds of activities involved can be confusing to sort out, but they consist generally of

• "Independent expenditures" by parties which involve the express advocacy of a clearly identified candidate's election or defeat. This is different from "issue advertising," which does not include "express advocacy," but the practical differences for parties may be limited.

• Independent expenditures by other political committees that are coordinated with parties.

• Other expenditures by political committees that are coordinated with parties—for example, expenditures for polling data, or for communications to the public on general political topics, or for voter registration or other voter contact activities.

• Coordination by parties with "outside groups" engaging in "issue advertising" or other forms of political action.

The Act intersects with existing law in various ways to limit the parties' actions in these various areas.

Party "independent" expenditures on behalf of their candidates

What is an "independent" expenditure?

Party involvement in "independent expenditure" activity is one front in the reform war. An independent expenditure is one made by a political committee or individual to expressly advocate the candidate's election or defeat, but without the candidate's cooperation or consent, and not at her request or suggestion. There is no dollar limit on truly independent expenditures. The Supreme Court, as it worked through the metaphysics of its decision in *Buckley v. Valeo*,[27] concluded that if money was spent truly independently of a candidate, then limits were not needed to address the danger, associated with ordinary contributions, of an illicit bargain with the candidate—a trade of contributions for official action.

Furious is a committed activist with ample amounts of money who decides that he must do what is possible to end the political career of Senator Smith. Working from his basement apartment alone, and without contact with Smith's opponent, or any other agent of Smith's opponent, he places orders for and pays for $2 million in "independent expenditures" calling for the "end to Smith's disgraceful career as our Senator: Vote to Replace Smith on November 5." Furious may spend without limit (though he must report these expenditures to the Federal Election Commission under "independent expenditure" reporting requirements").

The Court also held in *Colorado Republican* that the parties, like individuals and other political committees, could make independent expenditures on behalf of their own candidates.[28] With these "independent expenditures, the parties could escape the limits otherwise imposed on contributions made directly to their federal candidates, and "coordinated" expenditures made on their behalf. It appeared from the Court's rulings that parties could maintain independence from candidates for some purposes, and not for others. They might, for example, recruit candidates to run and train them, and offer them assistance along the way; but so long as they did not inform them or otherwise cooperate with them in planning and making a specific expenditure on their behalf, the expenditure was "independent" and the amount spent unlimited. The expenditure must be made from "hard" funds, and fully reported by the party.

Independent expenditures by political parties

A party recruits Congressional candidate Jackson. It meets with Jackson on her strategy for the race, helps her identify staff, and makes an early contribution to

---

[27] 424 U.S. 1 (1976).

[28] *FEC v. Colorado Republican Fed. Campaign Comm.*, 533 U.S. 431 (2001).

her campaign. In the general election, it becomes clear that Jackson is running into trouble, and needs more help than her campaign has funds to provide. The party, moreover, has little left under the limits for contributions to and coordinated expenditures on behalf of her campaign. So party officers meet without the knowledge of Jackson to plan a media campaign on her behalf, and fund it with $250,000 in "independent" expenditures. Jackson learns of the expenditures when the party's ads appear on the air, and its "independent" mail begins to arrive in mailboxes around the district. The party has made an "independent expenditure" and may spend freely in this way for Jackson without regard to the limit on contributions or party "coordinated" expenditures.

Background: distinguishing "independent expenditures" from "issue ads"

It is important to bear in mind how the Act has largely erased the once prominent distinction between an independent expenditure by a party and its "issue advertising." Under existing law, an "independent expenditure" must contain "express advocacy"—express advocacy of a clearly identified candidate's election or defeat—whereas an "issue ad" does not. The difference is between an appeal to "Throw Jones out" (independent expenditure) and "Call Jones and tell him that his bad votes on taxes are ruining our state"("issue ad"). Under existing law, the party running an issue ad could pay for it with both hard and soft money, while it must pay for an "independent expenditure" with hard money only. Under the new Act, both types of ads, if they refer to a clearly identified federal candidate, must be paid for with hard money. The only question is the one of coordination with the candidate: if the party has coordinated the ad with the candidate, then it must observe limits on how much it may pay for the ad under the law's "contribution" and "coordinated" spending limits.

An ad to the public states: "Congressman Jones lies like a rug. Call him and tell him to be honest for a change." This is not an independent expenditure. It is apparent that the ad sponsor dislikes Jones, but there is no mention in the ad of his election, or the wish of the sponsor, fairly inferred from the ad, that he lose it.

A national or state party must pay for with it hard money. If the party had "coordinated" the ad with the candidate, then dollar limits on the amount spent for the ad would apply. If the party ran the ad without coordination with a candidate, then no limits would apply to its spending for the ad.

The ad is modified to read: "Congressman Jones lies like a rug. Call him and tell him that you think it is time to change the carpeting." The FEC has developed rules on "express advocacy"[29] *which it would like to believe applies to an ad like this. After all, the agency reasons, who would not believe that the call to "change the carpeting," in an ad likening the candidate to a rug, is a call to remove him from office? The FEC has had limited success in persuading courts that this is "express advocacy": the Federal Circuit Court of Appeals for the Ninth Circuit agrees,*[30] *but other Circuits do not, and the Fourth Circuit has waged war on this view of the law.*[31]

The ad, modified once more, reads: "Congressman Jones lies like a rug. Call Congressman Jones and tell him to get out of town. And then, on November 5, make sure that he does." This is likely express advocacy.

Recognizing that parties may make independent expenditures, the Act's drafters were unhappy with the hybrid nature of the parties' relationship with their candidates—independent in some contexts, allowing for unlimited spending, while "coordinated" and subject to limits in other contexts. The Act therefore puts parties to a choice as soon as their federal candidates have been nominated. A party may make coordinated expenditures for their general election nominee, or independent expenditures on her behalf, but not both. The requirement kicks in when a nominee is chosen. Then the party must make the choice—it may choose to

Forcing parties to choose "independence"

---

[29] 11 C.F.R. § 100.22.

[30] *FEC v. Furgatch*, 869 F.2d 1256 (9th Cir. 1989)

[31] *FEC v. Christian Action Network*, 92 F.3d 1178 (4th Cir. 1996).

establish "independence" from the candidate, and spend unlimited monies on her behalf, or it may value instead the ability to work closely with the candidate and make only limited expenditures on behalf of the candidate on a "coordinated basis."

One party committee's choice binds all on the subject of "independence"

The Act puts this decision on the parties with some additional requirements intended to make it stick. It treats all committees of each party as a single committee for this purpose. So if the national committee of the Democratic Party chooses to make only coordinated expenditures on behalf of candidate X, its decision is binding on all other national committees—the congressional committees. The same holds true for state parties and all other district and local committees,[32] all of which are treated as a single committee, and any one of whom is bound under this provision by the decision made by another. The stated purpose of this provision was to safeguard true "independence" from a candidate by a party committee claiming it, by disallowing evasion through interactions with other party committees fully engaged with those same candidates.

A state party, considering how to proceed in supporting candidate X, decides that it will forego independence and make "coordinated" expenditures on his behalf within existing statutory limits. Once it has decided to do so, other district and local committees are saddled with that choice and may not make "independent" expenditures.

In addition, the Act provides that once a committee within the party structure decides to proceed with coordinated expenditures, it may not engage in certain transactions with another political party committee making (or intending to make) independent expenditures for the benefit of that candidate. The prohibited transactions consist of assigning the authority to make coordinated expenditures to that other committee;[33]

---

[32] 148 Cong. Rec. S2144 (daily ed. Mar. 20, 2002) (statement of Sen. McCain).

[33] This is something of a puzzle, because that other committee, once it decides to make independent expenditures, cannot make coordinated expenditures anyhow, on its authority or anyone else's.

transferring funds to that committee; or receiving any funds from that committee.[34]

Keeping the independent party committees apart from the others

This prohibition on interactions between party committees is aimed at efforts by a committee electing to coordinate with a candidate, to fund or support "independent" efforts by another party committee for that candidate. The Act makes the decision of any national committee the decision of all national committees, and in some way enforces against all state and local committees the decision of any one of them. As a result, the prohibition affects the relationship of national with state and local committees. It also is a broad prohibition, disallowing transfers of funds between party committees. This is the case even where the funds transferred are not intended for use on the race of the candidates on whose behalf the independent and coordinated spending is made or planned.

The state party foregoing "independence" from nominee X is offered funds from the congressional committee of the national party for its pending GOTV operation for the fall ticket. That congressional committee has resolved, however, to make independent expenditures for nominee X. As a result, the state party may not accept funds from the congressional committee, even if those funds are not intended for use in supporting nominee X.

There is an apparent hole in the Act's attempt to force parties to the choice between "independent" and coordinated spending, and it is opened by the parties' continued ability to finance "issue ads." As noted, there is only one material difference between the issue ad and the independent expenditure: the presence or absence of "express advocacy." If an issue ad is not coordinated, no limits apply to monies spent to air it—just as there are no limits on independent expenditures. So a party could elect to forego independence, and choose instead to make "coordinated" expenditures on behalf of its candidates, while also financing issue ads

---

[34] Note that political party committee may transfer unlimited "hard" funds between themselves under the existing law, and this legal allowance is not otherwise affected by the Act.

without limit for these same candidates' benefit. The issue ads would have to be paid for with hard money—but the same is true for any "independent expenditures" a party would finance.

Effects of coordinating with a party on independent spending for a candidate

No independence if a party is involved

The Act seeks to tighten the requirement of true independence for "independent expenditures" by individuals and political committees. It provides that they are not independent from candidates if they "coordinate" their spending with the candidate's political party. Existing law addresses only "coordination" with "any candidate, or any authorized committee or agent of such candidate." The Act brings parties explicitly into the picture, making clear that an expenditure cannot be independent if made "in concert or cooperation with or at the request or suggestion of...a political party committee or its agents." The drafters of the Act were apparently concerned to leave no ambiguity hovering over this point, and so it introduced parties directly into the definition. So in the example given of Mr. Furious, he may have avoided coordination with Smith's opponent, but his expenditure will not be "independent" if he coordinates his activities with the opponent's national, state or local party.

Wealthy Wilson discusses Jones' candidacy with his State Chair, and the two note that Jones is running low on television ad money, while his opponent is spending to beat the band. The Chair suggests to Wilson that he consider running ads of his own lauding Jones' sponsorship of federally funded pigeon waste disposal in public parks, and calling for his election. Wilson funds those ads. Under the Act, the expenditure would not be independent. Hence, Wilson would be treated as making a contribution to Jones, and it surely would have exceeded the limit (see below) of $2,000 per election.

But is this right? If one assumes that Jones is not privy to this discussion between the party Chair and Wilson, then the result wrought by the Act is a harsh one indeed. Jones is assumed to have received a contribution she did not request, as a result of a conversation that he did not authorize. The Act is more reasonably read to attribute Wilson's contribution to the party, not Jones. The unfairness is all the greater if the discussion between Wilson and the party chair is less explicit than presented in the hypothetical. The Chair may note that Jones is running out of money, and he might also supply Wilson with a copy of the law governing the "independence" of expenditures under the Act. But he may never actually invite the expenditure. What then? Time, rule-makings and litigation may answer the question.

Effects of coordinating other expenditures with parties

An additional limitation on political parties is concerned with their involvement in coordinating with political committees and other organizations their various other expenditures, not just independent expenditures. The existing law provides that expenditures—monies spent to influence the outcome of elections—will constitute contributions to candidates if made at their request or suggestion, or if made in cooperation, consultation, or concert with them. So if candidate Jones coordinates an expenditure with a political committee, in the hope, of course, that it will aid her candidacy, the expenditure when made would be treated as a contribution from the political committee to Jones.

In this section, the focus is on coordination with "political committees," not with outside groups. The term "political committee" means a committee that makes "contributions" and "expenditures" within the meaning of the existing law. Such a committee is registered with the FEC, discloses its finances, and complies with limits on what it receives and donates to candidates.

Candidate Jones approaches a political committee and proposes that it fund a mailing to residents of his district which would call into question the performance of Incumbent Gomes on budget policy. Existing law would suggest that any further expenditures made on this suggestion would result in a "contribution" from the committee to Jones. The committee, a multicandidate committee, may

*only make a contribution to Jones of $5,000 per election,
and any such contribution must be reported.*

**Parties
"coordinating"
with political
committees their
spending**

Political parties typically also communicate with other political committees about the prospects and mutual support of candidates. The Act provides that should a political party committee enlist the aid of such a committee in its projects—that is, should the party coordinate with the political committee in making an expenditure—the expenditure will be treated as a contribution to the party under the federal law.

So in the last example, Jones might not make the request to the political committee, but instead a committee of his political party might choose to do so. In that event, a contribution would still occur, but it would be a contribution to the party, not to Jones. The limits that apply are the limits on contributions from the political committee to the party; and the dollar amount of those limits depend on whether the party involved is a national, state or local committee. Thus a political committee that is a multicandidate committee under existing law may contribute $15,000 per calendar year to a national party committee, and $5,000 per calendar year to a state political party committee.[35] These limits, if invoked by way of a finding of "coordination', place real limits on communications and common action between and among the parties and all kinds of other political committees.

Party coordination with outside groups

The Act also takes up a large cause of recent years, that of the activities of outside groups—527s, or corporations, or tax-exempts—that benefit a candidate or party and may have been in some fashion "coordinated" with them. These groups are not political committees registered with the FEC and reporting under existing law. But they may produce voter guides, or "issue advertising," or other communications that plainly concern candidates and elections but are not treated as statutory campaign-related "expenditures." They may also propose these activities to candidates, or inform them

---

[35] These contribution limits are not changed under the Act.

of the activities; and the communications with the candidates may cover the content of the communications and the way they will be distributed.

The FEC in recent years has litigated the application of existing law to these activities and the case of note, so far shaping the law, has been *FEC v. Christian Coalition*.[36] There the Christian Coalition, which was not a political committee, funded and distributed voting records on incumbent officeholders who were also candidates for reelection. It communicated with certain of the affected candidates about these activities. The FEC claimed that these communications converted these "speech" activities into statutory, fully regulated expenditures. A court disagreed, acknowledging the communications with the candidates but generally holding that they fell short of triggering the restrictions of the federal campaign finance laws.

The FEC then proceeded to develop a rule based on the case, purporting to define when these communications for the benefit of candidates, and also "coordinated" with them, became a legal question of contributions, expenditures and reporting. The rule provides generally that these "communications" become "contributions and expenditures" if requested or suggested by the candidate, or if made after "substantial" discussion and negotiation about their content, timing, placement and other facets of distribution which results in "collaboration or agreement."

The FEC rule has made those unhappy with these types of "coordinated communications" unhappier still, on the ground that the rule is too permissive. The Act reflects these concerns, and requires that the Commission promulgate new rules to replace the existing ones. The Act does not supply the content of the new rule that it seeks to have promulgated. Instead it supplies a general principle, and also factors that the new rule should address.

The principle is hard-edged: it provides that the "regulations shall not require agreement or formal collaboration to establish coordination." Hence the new rule cannot depend on whether the candidate requests a particular communication, or works closely with the organization on

---

[36] *FEC v. Christian Coalition*, 52 F. Supp.2d 45 (D.D.C. 1999).

content and timing to bring it about. A subtle reference, a hint, an allusion—all of these may be enough to establish "coordination" between the candidate and the organization. Yet it cannot be known how broadly the rule might be drawn, until the Commission draws it.

Then there are additional factors that the rules are expected to address in some fashion. These are

(A) payments for the republication of campaign materials

(B) payments for the use of a common vendor

(C) payments for communications directed or made by persons who previously served as an employee of a candidate or political party

(D) payments for communications made by a person after substantial discussion about the communication with a candidate or political party.

The legislative history of this directive to the FEC does indicate that the Act's sponsors did not intend that coordination would occur "solely because the organization that runs such ads has previously had lobbying contacts with a candidate." [37]

This rulemaking requirement is addressed here, in a discussion of parties, though it also affects candidates. So in the section dealing with candidates, more on this topic will be said. The Act, however, proposes specifically to draw parties into the rule. The heading indeed of this section of the Act is "Coordination with Candidates or Political Parties." Moreover, the factors address "communications directed or made by persons who previously served as an employee of a candidate or a political party," and also any substantial discussion about a communication "with a candidate or a political party."

Coordinating "electioneering communications" with parties

The Act also addresses coordination between parties and other outside groups in the making of "electioneering communications." In simplest terms, but as will be discussed at length in the following section, an 'electioneering communication'; is one that refers to a federal candidate and is broadcast to a candidate's electorate within 30 days of a primary and 60 days of the general election. Think: "issue advertising" funded by 527s, corporations, tax exempts or unions. The Act

---

[37] 148 Cong. Rec. S2145 (daily ed. Mar. 20, 2002) (statement of Sen. McCain).

specifically provides that the "coordination" of these communications with parties will convert them into contributions to those parties. Of course, such a contribution is illegal, which is the point of the provision: to prohibit this coordination a national party committee.

Very Bad Corporation funds an "issue ad" which states "Senator Jones is a bonehead. Call him and tell him that he's a dummy." The ad is run on cable in the Senator's state 45 days before the general election It is an electioneering communication, and then the question is whether, in a meeting a day before the ad run, the corporation's lobbyist discussed the ad with Jones' opponent. The lobbyist acknowledges that he did inform the opponent of the ad, but that it was in no way coordinated with her. Now what? The FEC will have the first say, promulgating regulations to define coordination.

CONCLUSION

All told, the Act administers a considerable beating to the parties' current fundraising plans. Perhaps the parties may derive some comfort from the truth that this was not an accidental feature of the Act, but instead its primary purpose. At least, then, the Act does what those who wrote it intended for it to do. Their goal was to prohibit in some cases—those of the national parties—the raising and spending of soft money, and to severely limit this activity in other cases, namely, those of the state and local parties. Along the way, in the interest of tightening this soft money ban and guarding against loopholes, the Act places associated restrictions on fundraising and other actions of federal candidates and officeholders, party officers, and "agents" of parties. These restrictions go to how soft money is raised, while others—on tax exempts and 527s—go to how it may be spent.

Litigation is a sure thing. It has, in fact, been announced, in advance even of passage of the Act.[38] Members of Congress will participate in the litigation, as

[38] Ralph Z. Hallow, "McCain-Feingold Foe Says Senate Would Sustain Veto; Interest Groups Join Strategy Session," *Washington Times*, April 5, 2001 at A5.

will voters, donors, party members and some party organizations. They will claim that the restrictions and prohibitions of the Act violate the associational and speech rights under the First Amendment, affecting parties, candidates, party members and donors; and they are likely to complain, on equal protection grounds, that a statute concerned with soft money cannot treat parties for this purpose more harshly than it does outside groups.

Predictions about the course of litigation are surely foolish. The Supreme Court has ranged widely and somewhat inconsistently in recent years in its treatment of political parties. In some respects, they have fared well in claiming authority to structure their nominating processes as they wished, free of state interference.[39] Yet the government has been handed a large club with which to beat the parties on financing issues. In *FEC v. Colorado Republican Committee*, the second of two such cases, the Court, by a 5-4 vote, held that Congress could limit the amounts of money that parties could spend to support their candidates with "coordinated expenditures."[40] The Court made much of the alleged efforts of the party to help candidates avoid the contribution limits. The case concerned hard money limits, not alleged soft money abuses, and it might be thought that it has no bearing on the core attacks under the Act on party soft money. Yet, some could read the Court's opinion as a challenge to the proposition that parties occupied a position of honor or privilege within the political process, that they were for all intents and purposes not much different than any other private association collecting and spending funds for campaign-related purposes. The Act will test the Court's true sentiments on the subject, for it singles parties out within the scheme of restrictions and prohibitions on "soft money," and brings to full view the question of their relative standing and importance in the political process.

---

[39] *Cousins v. Wigoda*, 419 U.S. 477 (1975); *Democratic Party of the United States v. Wisconsin ex rel. La Follette*, 450 U.S. 107 (1981); *Tashjian v. Republican Party of Connecticut*, 479 U.S. 208 (1986); *California Democratic Party v. Jones*, 530 U.S. 567 (2000).

[40] *FEC v. Colorado Republican Fed. Campaign Comm.*, 533 U.S. 431 (2001).

CHAPTER 2

OUTSIDE GROUPS

Issue ads and other such activities funded by "soft money" are not the sole province of parties, but also the handiwork of outside groups. These groups, including so-called "527s," but also corporations, unions and trade associations, seek to avoid activities prohibited by the law or regulated by the FEC—those conducted with "express advocacy" or coordinated with candidates. The field of activities open to them is still wide. Their soft-money funded communications may include on-the-air-ads, but also phones, mail and even door-to-door advocacy on "issues" that may have a direct impact on voter choice in elections.[41]

The Act reflects a long-standing debate about the scope of permissible constitutional restraints on "outside group" political activity. The courts have shown a concern with the regulation of outside groups acting on their own and without express advocacy in funding "issue-related" communications. They have responded positively to the claim that these groups are engaged in speech, even if it is a form of speech effective in influencing collaterally the judgment of voters.[42] This position has influenced the development of the Act. Its approach to the limitation of the soft money activities of these groups is, accordingly, narrow and hedged with qualifications of one kind or another. The approach is therefore also complicated.

"Electioneering communications"
Just as a key term for parties is that of "federal election activity," so the key terms for outside groups are "electioneering communications" and "coordination." The coordination issues, arising from cases like the *Christian Coalition*, have been reviewed previously. It is sufficient

---

[41] David B. Magleby, ed., *Outside Money: Soft Money and Issue Advocacy in 1998 Congressional Elections (2000).*

[42] *FEC v. Central Long Island Tax Reform Immediately Comm.*, 616 F.2d 45 (2d Cir. 1980); *FEC v. Christian Action Network*, 92 F.3d 1178 (4th Cir. 1996); *Maine Right to Life Comm. v. FEC*, 98 F.3d 1 (1st Cir. 1996), *cert. denied*, 118 S.Ct. 52 (1997).

for the immediate purpose to stress that the FEC, and no doubt later the courts, will have to determine when an otherwise lawful communication on issues, free of express advocacy, becomes a "contribution" because it is "coordinated" with a candidate or party. In the meantime, the existing rule stands, providing that "coordination" occurs when the communications has been made at the request and suggestion of a candidate, or after "substantial negotiation" about its production, content, placement, timing and other such factors.

The Act proposes to impose certain disclosure requirements, but also some outright prohibitions, on "electioneering communications" by outside groups. The Act defines the term, and it makes clear that these are a special form of communication—made in a certain way, with a certain content, and directed toward a particular audience. The complete statutory definition:

(A) In General

Electioneering communication defined

(i) The term "electioneering communication' means any broadcast, cable, or satellite communication which
  (I) refers to a clearly identified candidate for federal office
  (II) is made within-
    a. 60 days before a general, special, or runoff election for the office sought by the candidate; or
    b. 30 days before a primary or preference election, or a convention or caucus of a political party that has authority to nominate a candidate, for the office sought by the candidate; and
  (III) in the case of a communication which refers to a candidate for an office other than President or Vice President, is targeted to the relevant electorate.

The definition does not include any particular content—other than that the ad "refer" to a "clearly identified candidate for federal office." The reference may be visual, or by name. There is, however, only one mode of communication affected by the provision—"broadcast, cable, or satellite communication." The restrictions attached to these "electioneering communications" do not apply, therefore, to a host of communications, such as those effected through the mails, the internet or the phones.

Moreover, the effective time period for these restrictions and prohibitions has been narrowed to 30 days prior to a primary and 60 days prior to the general, on the theory or assumption that ads of this kind "close" to an election have the undeniable purpose to influence the voters. Under the Act, a communication is targeted to the relevant electorate if it is received by 50,000 or more persons in the state or congressional district of the candidate "referred to."

The Act's concern with the broadcast of communications close to an election extends out into three directions. First, the Act compels certain disclosure of these activities by any "person"—which would include any corporation, union, partnership, 501(c) tax-exempt organization or "527." (This disclosure requirement does not fall on political committees reporting to the FEC, but they must in any event report all of their expenditures, including ones that would constitute "electioneering communications.") Second, the Act prohibits "electioneering communications" by corporations and unions. Third, the Act applies contribution limits—and in most respects, therefore, prohibits—any electioneering communications "coordinated" with any candidate or political party.

Sponsors of the Act made two principal arguments in support of these restrictions aimed at "electioneering communications"—or "issue advertising. First, they argued that the prohibition on corporate and union "electioneering communications" has "a basis in law extending back to 1907," when Congress imposed the standing prohibition on corporate spending in federal elections[43]. Second they argued that these issue ads had a clear connection to federal elections: they pointed to the frequency of such ads immediately before elections and to studies purporting to show that viewers interpreted these ads as intended to influence elections. Hence the argument is one of both purpose and effect: the timing and frequency of ads demonstrates their election influencing purpose while the reaction of viewers establishes

---

[43] 147 Cong. Rec. S3034 (daily ed. Mar. 28, 2001) (Statement of Sen. Snowe).

their election-influencing effect. Because the ads "are ultimately engulfing the political process," indeed "having a greater impact than the ads the candidates run themselves,"[44] the sponsors believed that the prohibitions and disclosure requirements are necessary to the enforcement of the campaign finance laws.

Reporting of "electioneering communications"

Reporting "direct" costs

The Act broadly requires reporting by any person who disburses monies for the "direct costs of producing and airing electioneering communications" which, in the aggregate, exceed $10,000 per year. The report—on forms the FEC will have to design in the future—will have to identify the person making the "disbursement" for this purpose, but also "any" person "sharing or exercising direction or control over the activities" of the organization and "the custodian" of the organization's books and accounts. Under this requirement, the report would include officers and directors of a corporation, or in the case of an association, the individuals holding formal responsibility for its direction. The report will also include:

• The organization's principal place of business;

• The amount of each disbursement of more than $200 for the "direct costs" of producing and airing the communication;

• The identification of the persons to whom the disbursements were made, which could include, for example, those engaged to produce the ad and the stations paid to air it;

• The "elections" to which the "electioneering communications pertain" and the names (if known) of the candidates;

Different reporting requirement for the use of only individual funds

The Act also adjusts the reporting requirements so that they apply more narrowly where the organization or association has established a "segregated bank account" to hold individual funds contributed for the purpose of financing these kinds of communications. In that case, the report need disclose only the names and addresses of contributors to that account who contributed a total amount of $1,000 or more over the period from the preceding calendar year through the date that the $10,000

---

[44] *Id.*

threshold for reporting was reached. Only American citizens or individuals admitted to permanent residency may contribute to this account.

The significance of this provision is that the organization may maintain other accounts for other purposes, but the amounts paid into and from those accounts would not be disclosed in the reports of electioneering communications. The segregated individual account would not be limited to the payment of electioneering communications, and could be used for other purposes, but it would be the only account whose contributors would be public disclosed in a report under the Act.

The Citizens for a Happier and More Fulfilling Existence fund electioneering communications, lauding Senator Jones on TV ads within 20 days of his primary election in his state. The organization pays $50,000 for the ads. The Citizens maintains a number of accounts and fund a number of activities, but for purposes of these ads, it maintains an account into which only individuals may contribute and from which these ads are financed. Its report to the FEC of these activities discloses only the activity from this account, and then only the amounts paid from the account for the "direct costs" of airing and producing these ads.

Later in the election, within 45 days of the general election, Citizens has run out of money in the segregated account, and draws funds for more of these ads from another account used for other organization activities. The next report filed under the Act must disclose all contributors to the organization, from all of its accounts, including others on which it did not draw for these electioneering communications.

Why all of this trouble? The sponsors were sensitive to the criticism that these reporting requirements fall on organizations that may, in fact, seeking only to comment on issues, albeit issues involving officeholders who are also candidates in a pending election. Their ads do not include "express advocacy," and the circumstances may be such that they are motivated by concerns other than that election. So the Act is limiting the range of disclosures which need to be made, focusing on "direct costs" and also affording organizations the opportunity to structure their accounts to limit the range of their finances subject to public disclosure.

Citizens for a Happier and More Fulfilling Existence are troubled by legislation sponsored by Senator Gloom brought to the floor for debate late in the Congressional session. As it happens, the debate and vote will occur within 60 days of the general election in which Gloom is standing for reelection but without an opponent. The Citizens begins to run advertisements intended to pressure Gloom into acceding to a particular, brightening amendment. The ad states: "Call Senator Gloom—Tell him to cheer up, and support the Goodcheer amendment." The ad cannot affect Gloom's reelection one way or other, and the organization's ad has been aired to advance a legislative objective. It must, however, file a report under the Act if the amounts spent for the ad exceed $10,000.

Admitting an intention to influence elections?

There is another wrinkle to the application of the disclosure requirements. The report under the Act compels disclosure in any such report of the "elections to which the electioneering communications pertain." An organization financing these ads will be reluctant to acknowledge that their ads "pertain" to any election. Their position will often be that they are seeking to influence the public policy debate, not to influence the outcome of elections. They will actively resist the claim that their purpose is election-related, because they will not concede the potential application of the federal campaign finance laws to their activities. And what does the term "pertain" mean for this purpose? If the ad does not make mention of an election—which it will not, precisely to avoid any possibility of "express advocacy"—then the question of whether the ads "pertain" to an election is a question about the organization's intention. Organizations may decline to answer the question, or answer it in the negative; and whether the FEC will insist on an answer could set up interesting conflicts and, perhaps inevitably, litigation.

The Act does provide for some exceptions from the reach of the term "electioneering communications," none of which will provide much comfort to organizations unhappy with these reporting requirements in the first instance. The Act does not apply these reports to communications by news organizations preparing them as part of a "news story, commentary, or editorial," unless the organization is "owned or controlled" by a political party, political committee or candidate. An exception is also provided for "candidate debates" sponsored under existing rules, and for any publicity for such debates.[45] The Commission is also authorized to provide, by rule, for other exemptions, though the authorization is highly if obscurely qualified. The Commission is allowed to add exemptions "to ensure the appropriate implementation" of the provisions governing "electioneering communications." The FEC is explicitly barred from promulgating an exemption for "issue advertising"—that is, "public communications" that refer to candidates and support or oppose, or promote or attack, those candidates.

What is not an "electioneering communication"?

Reports of "electioneering communications" must be filed within 24 hours of crossing the $10,000 threshold. Subsequent reports are filed for each additional spending in excess of each subsequent $10,000 trigger. The reports are filed with the FEC, which compiles the relevant information and makes it available on its website. The Act provides specifically that a contract to make disbursements will be treated as a disbursement for reporting purposes. So if an organization enters into a contract with a media firm to produce and place more than $10,000 in media which would qualify as "electioneering communications," the organization will have the obligation to report within 24 hours of executing that contract.

Timetable for reporting "electioneering communications"

The Citizens Committee finances research into Senator Jones' position on an issue. It expands the exercise to a full "opposition research report" which a consultant prepares for a cost of $15,000. So far no obli-

---

[45] The FEC rules allow news media corporations and tax-exempts to sponsor candidate debates, and allow corporations, unions and others to fund tax exempts' conduct of such events.

gation to report has been incurred: the monies spent so far, though they may be used later for electioneering communications, do not include the "direct costs" of producing and airing any such communications.

On the basis of this research, the Citizens Committee enters into a contract with a media firm to prepare and produce, and then buy the time for, electioneering communications. Those communications will state that Jones has a long history of sponsoring stupid legislation, and that those hearing or seeing the ad should call him and tell him to "wise up." If the agreement with the media firm calls for fees and costs exceeding $10,000, the Citizens Committee must prepare a report within 24 hours for filing with the FEC. A subsequent additional payment for airtime will generate another requirement for a report, also to be filed within 24 hours, if that additional payment exceeds $10,000.

Prohibiting corporate and union "electioneering communications"

The Act prohibits some "electioneering communications"; while compelling disclosure of all others. The prohibition is placed on those entities, and most pertinently corporations and unions, subject to the existing prohibitions on spending "in connection with a federal election." These entities may not fund electioneering communications, nor donate funds to another organization to finance them.

This prohibition raises the constitutional stakes of the Act considerably higher. The disclosure requirements present potential constitutional issues of their own, but here the Act absolutely prohibits a corporation from financing any broadcast, cable or satellite ad within the 30 and 60 day limits that refers to a federal candidate and is directed to the "relevant electorate." It is noted, however, that within these 30 and 60 day periods, the corporations and unions remain free to fund ads through other media, such as mail and telephone banks.

Powerful Corporation is angry over the proposed repeal of a tax provision which would have a significant impact on its business. As the Fall Congressional session winds down in an election year, Powerful launches advertisements in 15 states, attacking federal lawmakers from those states who have expressed support for the bill. The ads begin within 60 days of the general election.

Some the candidates named in the ad are running for reelection, though two are not: one announced her retirement, and the other lost in the primary. Some number of ads have run in states other than ones represented by these candidates, as part of the Company's interest in publicizing the issue. Those ads mention some of the candidates. Moreover, two of the candidates are United States Senators representing the same state, but only one is running this year, while the other—though a candidate for reelection—will not face the voters for another four years.

As it happens, moreover, Powerful has supported seven of these candidates earlier in the year with contributions from its PAC. The company's releases a statement announcing the ads which states that while it will continue to support most of these candidates for reelection, it is financing the ad blitz to focus their attention on the Company's extreme dissatisfaction with the tax measure. Under the Act,

• Powerful may run the ads in states other than ones represented by the candidates appearing in them. An electioneering communication is by definition one directed to the relevant electorate—a requirement not met by these ads.

• The Company may also run ads in states where the named federal officials are not candidates for reelection, either because of retirement or primary defeat.

• The Company, though otherwise Powerful, may not run the ads in states where the lawmakers mentioned are federal candidates, even if Powerful is otherwise supporting them for reelection.

• The Company may not run the ads refers to the United States Senator who is running for election in that year, but it may include in those ads his colleague who is a candidate but not on the ballot for another four years.[46]

Powerful Company will not be happy with these results, and one such company, union or other affected entity is sure to test the application of this provision in court. The Act anticipates this litigation, providing that if its definition of "electioneering communication" "is held to be constitutionally insufficient by final judicial decision," another definition, believed to be safer, should take its place. Just in case things go badly in court...

This alternative definition is similar to the structure of the party restrictions on "issue advertising," requiring not only the mention of a federal candidate but also language indicating support for or opposition to the candidate. Under the alternative, the communication would include language

Which promotes or supports a candidate for that office, or attacks or opposes a candidate for that office (regardless of whether the communication expressly advocates a vote for or against a candidate) and which also is suggestive of no plausible meaning other than an exhortation to vote for or against a specific candidate.

The language having to do with "no plausible meaning" has been drawn from an FEC rule, extracted in turn from a federal court decision, governing "express advocacy." [47] The FEC in years past sought out this rule to distinguish true campaign communications from others; it did not wish to have to depend on the presence of "magic words" like "vote," "elect," or "defeat." Its position has been in effect the old one of "If it walks and quacks like a duck, then a duck it must be"; and it will contend, further, that the failure to call a duck a duck will encourage people to duck the law and contribute to the same erosion experienced in the existing law.

Critics of the Act's approach to "electioneering communications," however, are unlikely to be assuaged by this substitute language which they will attack as still vague and uncertain in its application, and therefore ineffective in distinguishing regulated campaign

---

[46] "The reference to a clearly identified candidate is intended to mean a candidate who is up for election in that two-year cycle. Therefore, if one Senator is up for election in a cycle, an ad that appears within 60 days of an election and mentions only the second Senator for that state is not an electioneering communication, even though the second Senator is also technically a candidate for election some years hence." Statement of Supporters of the Bipartisan Campaign Reform Act of 2001 Concerning Intent of Certain Provisions. 147 Cong. Rec. S3245 (daily ed. Apr. 2, 2001).

[47] See *Furgatch*, 869 F.2d 1256 (9th Cir. 1989).

activity from protected speech. They will argue that an "attack" on an officeholder who is a candidate is still an attack on an officeholder, and that if the attack is focused on official acts without any accompanying "express advocacy," there is no basis for interference from the campaign finance laws. And it will not help, they would argue, to add that the attack must be "suggestive" of "no plausible meaning" other than an appeal to vote one way or another on candidacy. "Suggestive" to whom, and who judges the "plausibility" of the alternative meaning? Since the answer is that the government (FEC) is the judge in the first instance of the application of these terms, those believing that the government's role in politics must be both limited and clearly defined will find the result unappealing.

The constitutional sensitivities associated with the prohibition of "electioneering communications" appear also in a provision ostensibly exempting in certain respects 501(c)(4) tax-exempt and "527" political organizations. The Act appears to allow them to make "electioneering communications" so long these are "paid for exclusively by funds provided directly by individuals who are United States citizens or nationals or lawfully admitted for permanent residence" under federal immigration laws. The emphasis here is on the term "exclusively": the exception is lost if any portion of the cost of the communication is paid directly or indirectly from corporate or union funds. Moreover, if the 501(c)(4) tax exempt receives business income, or donations from corporate or union sources, it must establish a separate segregated account holding only individual contributions from which the full cost of the electioneering communication must be paid.

Exempting 501(c) and 527 organizations?

The exception turns out to be "fool's gold"—the opposite in substance than a quick first impression might suggest. The Act disallows the exception if the communication is "targeted" to the relevant electorate. As noted previously, this is not a matter of intention: a communication is "targeted to the relevant electorate" if it can be received by 50,000 or more persons in the state or Congressional District of the candidate in the ad.

Answer: "no"

---

[48] 147 Cong. Rec. S2846 (daily ed. Mar. 26, 2001) (statement of Sen. Wellstone).

Different Types of Political Actors: Different Legal Requirements [49]

	Reg. as "Political Committee" and Reporting to FEC	Limits on Contributions Received	Prohibitions on "Soft Money"	Reporting of Soft Money Activity to FEC
National Party Committees	YES	YES	YES	N/A – cannot accept any
State & Local Party Committees	YES – if active in federal elections	YES – under federal & state law	YES – for "federal election activity"	YES
"527s"	NO – unless contributes to federal candidates or engages in "express advocacy"	NO – Unless contributes to federal candidates or engages in "express advocacy"	NO – except if incorporated, cannot make broadcast "electioneering communications"	YES – for broadcast "electioneering communications"
Tax-Exempts (501)(c)(4)s	NO	NO	NO – except if incorporated & making "electioneering communications"	YES – for broadcast "electioneering communications"
Federal Candidates Committees	YES	YES	YES	N/A – cannot accept any
State Candidate Committees	NO	YES – if imposed by state law	NO – except if engaged in certain "federal election activity"	YNO – but under state law
Corporations and Unions	NO – but their PACs might	NO – except their PACs	NO – except for electioneering communications	YES – for broadcast "electioneering communications"
Federally Registered Political Committees or PACs	YES	YES – under federal and state laws	Must allocate hard & soft money for get-out-the-vote & other activity under FEC rules	YES – under state laws and FEC rules

49 General rules: there are always exceptions.

As a general rule, the Act puts, then, these organizations on the same footing as all others subject to the prohibition on corporate electioneering communications. The organizations may run these ads without restriction (though with disclosure) anywhere but the states or districts where the federal candidates are named. But so may any corporation or union subject to this prohibition. And to the extent that the prohibition kicks in when "targeting" occurs, it kicks in for these other organizations—for 501(c) tax-exempts, as well as for-profit corporations or unions. This "exception" that is not an exception results from an amendment adopted by the Senate, intended to make sure that "the same rules and prohibitions [as they 'affect electioneering communications"] that apply to corporations and unions apply to all the other interest groups." [48]

It is emphasized that the prohibition on "electioneering communications" falls on unions and corporations, or on communications paid with union or corporate funds. An *unincorporated* 527 or tax-exempt organization is not subject to the prohibition, so long as neither a corporation or a union "directly or indirectly disburses any amount for any of the costs of the communication." It would appear, though it is not completely clear, that an unincorporated 527 or tax-exempt could accept unions or corporate funds for other purposes, provided that it paid the costs of any "electioneering communication" out of individual funds held in a separate segregated account. It is clear that individuals and federal political committees may pay for ads in the form of "electioneering communications" at any time.

The targeting restriction focuses on Congressional races, excluding presidential campaigns. An electioneering communication run anywhere in the United States will be seen or heard by members of the presidential electorate. The prohibition operates absolutely in this instance, triggered by an ad wherever it is run that refers to a presidential candidate within the 30- and 60-day time periods before primary and general elections.

Increases in the contribution limits

FROM ∨ TO->	Senate cand	House cand	Presidential	Nat'l party cand	State party cmte	PAC	Ann agg lmt
Individual	$2,000/elec	$2,000/elec	$2,000/elec	$25,000/cal yr	$10,000/cal yr	$5,000/cal yr	$95,000/2 yrs[2]
Multicandidate PAC	$5,000/elec	$5,000/elec	$5,000/elec	$15,000/cal yr	$5,000/cal yr	$5,000/cal yr	n/a
Non-multicandidate PAC	$2,000/elec	$2,000/elec	$2,000/elec	$25,000/cal yr	$10,000/cal yr	$5,000/cal yr	n/a
National party committee	$35,000 [1]	$5,000/elec	$5,000/elec	Unlimited	Unlimited	$5,000/cal yr	n/a
State party committee	$5,000/elec	$5,000/elec	$5,000/elec	Unlimited	Unlimited	$5,000/cal yr	n/a
Non-individual "person" (e.g., partnerships, Indian tribes)	$2,000/elec	$2,000/elec	$2,000/elec	$25,000/cal yr	$10,000/cal yr	$5,000/cal yr	n/a

[1] Specifically, the DSCC/DNC and NRSC/RNC may respectively give a combined $35,000 to each Senate candidate during the calendar year in which the election is to be held.

[2] The application of this limit is complex: see discussion at p. 70.

CHAPTER 3

LESS SOFT MONEY, MORE HARD MONEY: INCREASES IN THE FEDERAL CONTRIBUTION LIMITS

A s originally introduced in the Senate, the Act did not provide for any broad adjustment upwards in the limits on "hard money" or federal contributions. It did raise the limit on contributions from individuals to state parties from $5,000 to $10,000 per calendar year. This increase was fashioned in the belief that as national party committees lost their "soft money" sources, the state parties would be compelled to "pick up the slack"—to raise more money for various activities that national parties for some time had funded. Supporters also noted that inflation had severely eroded the effective purchasing power of the $1,000 per election contribution limit for individuals, enacted into federal law in 1974.[50] With greater responsibilities, the state parties would need more resources, and as the overall emphasis of the bill is to restrict all party soft money activities, the Act sought to provide those additional resources in the form of increased "hard money" contributions.

The Senate debate resulted in two amendments which substantially broadened that approach, increasing contributions across-the-board for Senate candidates and party committees and increasing them still more in one special case. The special case was that of the Senate candidate facing an opponent who commits substantial amounts of his her own money to the race. In that latter case, the Senate adopted a "millionaire's amendment," modified and passed also by the House for Congressional races as well, intended to provide increased limits for a candidate facing heavy personal spending by a wealthy opponent.

More money for candidates and parties— and to battle millionaires, too

Increases in the contribution limits
The chart on the next page sets out the changed limits. It also notes that the Act "indexed" some of the limits for

---

[50] "Thirty years ago, a car cost $2,700. Now it costs $22,000. The cost of campaigning has risen even more dramatically....Virtually every aspect of campaigning, from the salaries for consultants to the paper on which you write—all of it is much more expensive today." 147 Cong. Rec. S2459 (daily ed. Mar. 19, 2001) (statement of Sen. Feinstein).

inflation, but not others: the indexed limits appear in italics. The chart does not address the significant additional limit increases provided for under the millionaire amendment, but these are discussed below, with examples.

Candidates and parties make off with the prize, while PACs—political committees established by unions, corporations, and trade associations, and other political committees which are not political party committees—did not receive a raise in their limits. Limits on individual contributions to candidates and state parties are doubled—to $2,000 per election in the first case, and to $10,000 in the second. The contribution limit for individuals contributing to national party committees was increased by 25%, from $20,000 per calendar year to $25,000.

The complicated aggregate limit on individual contributions

The Act also raised the aggregate annual limit for contributions, from $25,000 per calendar year now, to $95,000 over a two-year election cycle, running from January 1 of an odd-numbered year through December 31 of the next, even-numbered year. But as discussed in Chapter 1, the limit in application is somewhat complicated.

Of the $95,000
- $37,500 may be contributed to candidates (in amounts of $2,000 per candidate per election)
- the balance of $57,500 is available for contribution to other committees, such as party committees, or political committees established by corporations, unions, or just citizens banding together to express a common political agenda (e.g. Citizens Banding Together to Express a Common Political Agenda). BUT...
- ONLY $37,500 of the balance of $57,500 may be contributed to political committees which are not national party committees.

Donor Wilson wishes to give as much she possibly can in the 2004 cycle. To do so, she cannot exceed $37,500 in contributions to candidates, and she must make at least $20,000 in contributions to national party committees.

Donor Smith is a party enthusiast. He makes the full amount of contributions he is allowed to candidates. Now he wishes to contribute the balance available under

the aggregate limit, $57,500, to national party commit-
tees. He may do so. Of the $57,500, $20,000 is reserved
for the national party committees; but he could
contribute the full amount of $57,500, if he wished, to
national party committees.

There are other complexities, perhaps also anom-
alies, in the construction of the revised contribution
limits. As noted, certain of the limits are indexed for
inflation. These include the limits to candidates and
national party committees, and also the aggregate limit
of $95,000 per two-year election cycle on all hard
money, federal contributions. These increases become
effective in January of the odd-numbered year—2003
for the 2004 election cycle. The FEC does not normally
have the Consumer Price Index data until March
following an election. So some period of time will pass
after each election when the limits will, for legal
purposes, have increased, but the precise amount of the
limit will not be known.

The timing of indexing

Differences in indexing may also have other effects of
interest. Under the law governing public funding of
presidential candidates, the government may match
$250 of an individual contribution received by an eligi-
ble presidential candidate. This amount is not,
however, indexed, and so as the individual contribution
limits increase, the "matchable" amount for presidential candidates seeking public funds will decline as a
percentage of the total contribution made.

Indexing: No help to presidential public funding system

Another result of the approach to indexing is the
difference in the treatment of "multicandidate" and
regular political committees. A multicandidate PAC is a
committee that qualifies by the breadth of its activities
for a higher limit on contributions to candidates: $5,000
rather $1,000 per election. It qualifies for the special
limit by filing with the Commission a certification that
it has been registered with the Commission as a political committee for at least 6 months, that it has made
contributions to at least 5 federal candidates and that
it has received contributions from more than 50
persons. A committee that does not so qualify is limited
to the $1,000 per election limit. The Act indexes the

Indexing some PACs, but not others

nonmulticandidate limit, but not the multicandidate limit, with the result that at some time in the future indexing may power an increase in the lower, nonmulticandidate limit beyond the limit enjoyed by the multicandidate committee.

"Persons" have their own limit

The increase in limits also affects "persons," as well as individuals. Persons as defined under the law may contribute up to $2,000 per election to any candidate, and they also enjoy the same authority as individuals to give under the increased limits $25,000 in a calendar year to national party committees and $10,000 to state parties. Under the law, "persons" include partnerships, certain limited liability companies, Indian tribes, and multi-candidate political committees. The terms under which these "persons" may contribute are not the same, though the subject is not one for treatment here. Certain of these "persons" run up against other limitations in making federal contributions, and some—like certain limited liability companies that are taxed as corporations and thus treated like corporations for purposes of the campaign finance law—may not contribute at all.

Protection against millionaires?

The individual limits—and also in some instances the party spending limits—have also been increased under the "millionaire's" amendment, to lighten the stresses on a candidate faced with a wealthy opponent willing to commit substantial sums of money to the competition. The sponsors of the amendment in the Senate acknowledged, rightly, that the provision is "very complicated."[51] There are moreover different provisions affecting Senate and House candidates, though they are structured conceptually much the same. The similarities in approach are critical to appreciating what the amendment is designed to accomplish, and how it works.

First, each of the provisions provides a method for determining when the increase in the contribution limits is triggered. In both cases, the trigger is the stated intention of a wealthy opponent to spend from personal funds in an election in excess of a "threshold

---

[51] 147 Cong. Rec. S2542 (daily ed. Mar. 20, 2001) (statement of Sen. Domenici).

amount." This amount is calculated differently, as one would assume, for the House and Senate: in the House, the number is $350,000, while the Senate provision keys the amount to the voting age population of the state.

Second, each of the provisions makes the increase of the limit depend, in part, on how much money the candidate facing the wealthy opponent has committed from his or her own personal funds and how much she maintains in the way of an advantage in cash from other contributors. These calculations are intended to gear the relief to the candidates who really need it—not candidates who, in some combination of personal spending and fundraising, remain competitive even with a wealthy opponent.

Third, each of the provisions identifies different amounts of contribution limit increases available to candidates with "millionaire" opponents. The House offers a tripled limit, and also removes the limit on party "coordinated" spending for the candidate with a wealthy opponent. The Senate provides for a graduated series of increases, and only for an exemption from party committee spending for the candidate facing the most massive level of personal spending by a wealthy opponent.

Fourth, each of the provisions defines the terms under which the increased limits are suspended. The suspension of the limit in both instances occurs when the wealthy candidate withdraws, or if the amount of contributions received under the increased limits exceeds a percentage of the wealthy candidate's spending,[52] or if the candidate's own personal spending increases to a certain level.

Fifth, each of the provisions compels the candidate who receives increased limits to return to the donors, after the election, the amounts raised under these limits that have not been used.

Sixth (and last), each provision has a related provision that prohibits a candidate who spends more than $250,000 from his personal funds in an election from raising contributions after the election to repay himself.

---

[52] The sponsors of the amendment term this limit a "proportionality provision," which is a means of "ensuring that a wealthy candidate is not punished by the less wealthy candidate's ability to raise funds" under increased contribution limits. 147 Cong. Rec. S2542 (daily ed. Mar. 20, 2001) (statement of Sen. DeWine).

This is the basic scheme, and the details are probably most clearly presented by separating out the treatment of the House and Senate, and showing with an example for each case how a candidate considering the opposition of a wealthy candidate would determine whether she might have the advantage of increased individual, and perhaps also party spending limits, under these provisions. The provisions use specialized terms for some of the key steps, and these are mentioned if only to introduce them to readers who may, if the provision sustains court scrutiny, hear them uttered in the future.

Senate elections. The "threshold amount" is the amount spent by an opponent of personal funds that brings into play the potential for an increase in the limits for the affected candidate. A candidate determines this amount by multiplying $0.04 times the relevant state's voting age population, and adding $150,000.

Notification of spending

Within 15 days after becoming a candidate, the wealthy opponent must file a declaration with the FEC and with the other candidates in the race, stating the amount of personal funds she intends to spend in excess of the threshold amount. ("Personal funds" includes bank loans secured against a candidate's personal assets.) This is a simply a declaration of intention, which does not trigger access to the higher limits. But at the time the opponent makes or obligates to make expenditures from personal funds totaling more than two times the "threshold amount" in any particular election, she must file another notification, with the FEC and with the opposing candidate, within 24 hours. Additional notifications are required within 24 hours after each additional $10,000 in expenditures from personal funds.

Now that the battle lines are drawn, and the wealthy opponent has made her move by the requisite amount over the threshold, the candidate may proceed to calculate the increase in the contribution limit to his campaign from individuals. This occurs in several steps—so hang on:

Calculating the disadvantage

1. The candidate must calculate the so-called" opposition personal funds" amount. This is the largest total of personal fund expenditures made in the election by the wealthy opponent, MINUS (a) the amount of personal funds the candidate has used in the same elec-

tion and (b) any additional advantage the candidate with the wealthy opponent may have in other fundraising. This fundraising advantage is known in the Act as the "gross receipts advantage." It is calculated from June 30 and December 31 off-year fundraising totals, and it is the difference between 50% of the candidate's cycle-wide gross receipts and 50% of opponent's cycle-wide gross receipts (not including personal funds).

Wealthy Wilson has raised $1.8 million by the end of the off-year, that is, as of December 31, while her opponent, Modesty Means, has raised $4.0 million. In determining the so-called "opposition personal funds amount"—which in turn will decide the availability and amount of increased limits for Modesty Means—the $1.1 million advantage Modesty Means enjoys in general fundraising is debited against Wilson's personal spending (50% of Modesty's $4 million minus 50% of Wealthy's $1.8 million, or $2 million minus $900,000). This lower net number will reduce the availability and amount of increased contributions limits for Means, because while she is being outspent in personal funds, she is making up the difference to the some extent with her general fundraising advantage.

2. Now the candidate may proceed to calculate the level of increased contribution limit, by figuring out the multiple by which the "opposition personal funds" amount exceeds the "threshold amount":

Calculating the increased contribution limit for responding to the millionaire

• if the "opposition personal funds" amount is 2 times to 4 times the "threshold amount," then the limit is multiplied by 3 ($6,000 per individual per election).
• if the "opposition personal funds" amount is 4 times to 10 times the "threshold amount," then the limit is multiplied by 6 ($12,000 per individual per election).
• if the "opposition personal funds" amount is 10 times or more the "threshold amount," then the candidate's party may make unlimited coordinated expenditures on his behalf.

The candidate provided with these increased limits is not, once qualified, perpetually eligible to raise at the higher limits and benefit from unlimited coordinated

When the limit comes down again....

expenditures. The limits decline from the higher level when: (i) the candidate spends personal funds in a way that would change the calculations, (ii) the opponent who triggered the higher limits drops out, or (iii) the amount by which the candidate benefited from higher individual contribution limits or party spending limits exceeds 110% of the "opposition personal funds" amount.

Giving back after the election what was not spent When the election is over, the candidate must determine the amount raised but not spent under increased limits, and then refund the excess portions to the original donors within 50 days after the election.

> *Booker, a librarian, is running for Senate in Bedford Falls against Potter, a wealthy banker. The state's voting age population is 100,000, making the "threshold amount" for personal spending $154,000.*
>
> *Both Booker and Potter win their primaries. Shortly thereafter, Potter puts $2 million of his own funds into the race, and files a notice with Booker and the FEC. Booker pulls out her adding machine. So far, she has put none of her own money into the campaign, and Potter has outraised her. As a result, the "opposition personal funds" amount is $2 million, or more than 10 times the "threshold amount" of $154,000. Booker can thus accept up to $12,000 for the general election from an individual. Her party can also make unlimited coordinated expenditures on her behalf.*
>
> *Yet before Booker can spend any of the extra money she has raised, Bedford Falls is rocked by an embezzlement scandal at Potter's bank. Potter withdraws from the race after being forced to admit that he perjured himself before federal regulatory authorities.*
>
> *After watching Potter's press conference on TV, Booker immediately directs her campaign to stop raising funds at the higher limits, and the national party stops making coordinated expenditures above the normal limit. An unknown and poorly funded candidate replaces Potter on the ballot in November, and Booker wins overwhelmingly without having to spend much money at all. Before Christmas, her campaign issues refunds to the donors who contributed at the higher limits that she briefly enjoyed because of Potter's personal funds.*

House elections. The differences between the House

and Senate approaches are straightforward, even if in application, the amendment is complex. The House threshold amount is $350,000 in any particular election, and the candidates planning to spend in excess of this amount must file a notification with the FEC, the opponent, and each national party within 24 hours. They must file additional notifications within 24 hours after each additional $10,000 in expenditures.

The calculation of opposition personal funds is the same for House and Senate candidates, and if it exceeds $350,000 for the House candidate, the individual limit is tripled for that candidate, and her party may also make unlimited coordinated expenditures on her behalf. Continued eligibility for the increased limits will depend, as in Senate elections, on the candidate's use of her own personal funds, and on the continued candidacy of the wealthy opponent. The House provision, like the Senate provision, also limits the amount of monies raised under the increased limit to a specified percentage of the wealthy opponent's "opposition personal funds" amount. The House limit, however, is lower—100%, rather than the 110% limit set by the Senate provision. As with the Senate, the House candidate, like the Senate candidate, must also calculate after the election the amount raised under the increased limits but left unspent, and then refund the excess portions to the original donors within 50 days.

Jed Leland, a former reporter, is running for Congress in New York City in the Democratic primary against Charles Foster Kane, a wealthy publisher. In the closing days of the campaign, Kane takes a $500,000 personal loan, secured against his lavish Florida vacation home, and puts the funds into his campaign. He files the required notice with Leland and the FEC.

As of December 31 of the previous year, Leland had raised $1,000,000 to Kane's $900,000. The son of wealthy parents himself, Leland had also loaned $100,000 to his campaign. As a result, Leland's "opposition personal funds" amount is $350,000: Kane's $500,000 in personal spending, minus the sum of: (a) Leland's $50,000 gross receipts advantage (50% of Leland's $1 million raised minus 50% of Kane's $900,000, or $500,000 minus $450,000) and (b) Leland's own $100,000 in personal spending.

Because Leland's "opposition personal funds" does not exceed $350,000, he cannot raise at higher limits. Kane crushes Leland in the primary.

The millionaire's provisions are unlike any provision of federal campaign finance law throughout its history. The FEC will be busy with rules to implement their terms. Candidates have special reporting obligations, and also calculations to make on which the allowance of increased limits is based; and the FEC will likely produce forms and otherwise guide candidates in the performance of these tasks.

No doubt, too, the FEC will arbiter disputes over compliance with these provisions. Has the person planning large personal expenditures made timely notification of the intent, and then also of the expenditures? Has a candidate raised more money under increased limits than the eligibility rules allow? Did a candidate properly calculate monies received under these increased limits and make timely post-election refunds to the donors?

Conclusion on the "millionaire" amendment

These provisions will also likely be among those contested in post-enactment litigation, as litigants raise the question of whether this sort of "special case" adjustment is permissible anyhow for some candidates—those facing millionaires—and not others. This question will likely be raised against the background of the Act's focus on the danger of corruption associated with large questions. Critics may question how the Act might plausibly limit contributions to $2,000 per election, on the grounds that a larger amount would risk corruption, while authorizing contributions substantially larger for a candidate facing a millionaire. If a contribution exceeding $2,000 risks corruption, then, they would argue, it will presumably do so regardless of the reasons why a candidate needs the money. In fact, a candidate who urgently needs the money to counter the resources of a wealthy opponent, stands to incur an even larger measure of indebtedness to the donor who lends a monied hand in the hour of need. And still another question of interest may be whether Congress can enact special provisions designed to discourage, or mitigate the impact, of personal spending for election related purposes that the Supreme Court has held to be constitutionally protected.

Other contribution or fundraising limits and prohibitions

The Act makes some other changes to the rules governing the making and solicitation of contributions in federal elections. They are varied, unified only as parts of an overall attempt by the drafters to plug up one perceived hole or the other in existing law.

One provision amends a longstanding prohibition of the criminal code on "fundraising on federal property." Existing law stated that

> It shall be unlawful for any person to solicit or receive any contributions…in any room or building occupied in the discharge of official duties by any [Members of Congress, candidates for Congress, officers or employees of the United States, or persons receiving any salary or compensation for services from the US Treasury], or in any navy yard, fort or arsenal.

The provision was amended in 1979 to allow Congressional staff to accept contributions sent to them in their offices, but not solicited for delivery there, provided that the contributions were transferred within seven days to their employers' political committees.

For some time, it lay dormant, surfacing from time to time when the Justice Department would address apparent violations resulting from "computer-generated direct mail campaigns in which solicitation letters are inadvertently sent to prohibited areas."[53] The Department, concluding that "[S]uch matters do not warrant prosecution," would simply advise the mailer that its fundraising lists should be purged of federal government addresses. Attention turned back to this provision, however, when allegations were made against the reelection effort of President Clinton, focusing specifically on the alleged use of White House "coffees" and other events and facilities to raise funds.[54]

The Act amends the provision to clarify the different

Fundraising on federal property

---

[53] Craig C. Donsanto and Nancy S. Stewart, U.S. Department of Justice, *Federal Prosecution of Election Offenses* at 68-69 (6th ed. 1995).

paths taken by the prohibition. First, it prohibits "any person" from soliciting or receiving contributions from a person located in a federal government office. Second, it turns the other direction and applies the prohibition to an individual who is an officer or employee of the federal government, barring them from such solicitations or receipts "while in any room or building" used for federal government business. This revised provision removes any confusion about the applicable legal authority, which had been read to prohibit solicitations only when the prospective donor was on government property.

The amended prohibition retains the prospects for both a criminal penalty and fine, but limits the fine to $5,000. The amendment retains the allowance for inadvertent receipt of monies on federal property, conditioned on their transfer within seven days to a political committee, and it extends the allowance to contributions received in the Executive Office of the President.

Contributions by foreign nationals

The 1996 Presidential election fundraising controversies make their appearance also in a provision "strengthening" the ban on foreign nationals in federal elections. For some time, some question was raised and debated about the scope of the prohibition, and specifically about whether it extended to contributions of "soft money" to political parties.[55]

The "strengthening" amendment of the Act is meant to leave no doubt about the breadth of the prohibition. The foreign national prohibition now applies to "donations," not only to "contributions"—so it is not relevant that the foreign national or party claims that the purpose of the funds was to influence a nonfederal rather than a federal election. The Act specifically applies the prohibition to contributions or donations to political party committees, or to expenditures or independent expenditures, or to disbursements for "electioneering communications."[56]

---

[54] Investigation of Illegal or Improper Activities in Connection with 1996 Federal Election Campaigns, Final Report of the Comm. on Gov't Affairs, S. Rep. No. 105-167, at 191-223 (1998).

[55] A District Court held that it did not apply to soft money, only to "hard money" contributions to candidates or to the hard "federal" accounts of parties. A Court of Appeals reversed on this issue. *United States of America v. Kanchanalak*, 192 F.3d 1037 (D.D.C. 1999).

The Act amends existing law by absolutely prohibiting contributions, hard and soft, by minor children (17 years old or younger). Existing law allowed minors under 18 to contribute, on the condition that 1) the contribution decision was made knowingly and voluntarily by the minor child; 2) the funds (or goods and services) contributed are the minor child's, such as funds from a trust established for and in the child's name; and 3) the contribution was not made from a gift donated to the child to make the contribution possible, or from other funds controlled by another person. Under the Act, a minor cannot contribute at all, under any circumstances, to a candidate or to a political party. Whether a well-heeled, politically informed child can overturn this restriction in court remains to be seen.[57]

No contributions by minor children

A final change of interest is the Act's amendment of the existing law prohibition on "fraudulent misrepresentation of campaign authority." This provision dates back to early Watergate controversies, and it is concerned with "dirty tricks" which occur when a candidate for federal office, or the employee or agent of such a candidate,

Fraudulent fundraising

> Fraudulently misrepresent[s] himself or any committee or organization under his control as speaking or writing or otherwise acting for or on behalf of any other candidate or political party...on a matter which is damaging to such other candidate or political party...

The Act does not change this prohibition, but it adds another one intended to prevent the fraudulent solicitation of funds. This change is concerned with individuals and organizations carrying or using the name of candidates or parties without their permission to conduct fundraising appeals.[58]

---

[56] An "electioneering communication," it will be recalled, refers to a federal candidate in any broadcast, cablecast or satellite media within 30 days of a primary or 60 days of a general election.

[57] Unlike the case of foreign nationals, the prohibition is not extended to funds donated to support "electioneering communications." Perhaps the younger set will look in that direction for the expression of their political interest.

[58] See *Friends of Phil Gramm v. Americans for Phil Gramm in '84*, 587 F. Supp 769 (E.D. Va. 1984).

CHAPTER 4

RESTRICTIONS ON FEDERAL CANDIDATES AND OFFICEHOLDERS

In the chapter on parties, there appeared some discussion of the prohibitions on federal candidates' and officeholders' solicitation, receipt, direction, transfer, or expenditure of "soft money" in connection with an election for federal office. Those prohibitions apply to the candidates' fundraising for both national, state and local political parties. There are exceptions, some of which have been noted, such as the allowance for federal candidates or officeholders to speak, attend or be a featured guest at a state party event held to raise "soft money," or to raise money under restrictions for charities engaged in election-related work, such as GOTV and voter registration.

There are still additional restrictions that require attention.

These restrictions apply to:

• "Agents" of candidates and officeholders

• An entity directly or indirectly established, financed, maintained or controlled by or acting on behalf of 1 or more candidates or individuals holding federal office.

The Act does not explain how someone might become an "agent" of an officeholder or candidate for the purposes of these restriction—just as it did not explain "agency" in the provision prohibiting party soft money activity. Moreover, unlike those party provisions, the ones involving candidate or officeholders do not require that to be an "agent," an individual must be "acting on behalf of" the candidate or officeholder when engaged in the prohibited activity. Whether this definitional difference was intended or inadvertent, it could have real consequences. An individual who was an "agent" of a candidate in any capacity could be prohibited from undertaking the soft money activities forbidden to the candidate.

Who is the 'agent' of a federal officeholder or candidate?

Stanley is the administrative assistant to Congressman Jones, and maintains strong ties to state party organiza-

*tions in the Congressman's state. For years, he has moon-
lighted as an adviser to the party on fundraising and strategy. After the Act passes, it appears that Stanley may not
encourage party supporters to make soft money contributions to the party. It may not matter whether Congressman
Jones has directed his aide to encourage these contributions: as an agent of the Congressman, he may be separately
enjoined from the same activities forbidden to his boss.*

"Leadership PACs"

Then there is the matter of "leadership PACs," which
are multicandidate committees closely associated with
and typically led by federal officeholders. Those PACs,
unlike the personal campaign committees of these
officeholders, do not expend funds to support their
reelection, but rather raise funds with their assistance
for distribution to other candidates. These PACs will
often have both federal and nonfederal accounts, drawing on the nonfederal accounts for contributions under
state law to state and local candidates. Those soft
accounts also defray a part of the costs of the adminis-
tration and fundraising of these PACs.

**No soft
money for
Leadership
PACs?**
Under the Act, a federal officeholder would be prohibited from soliciting or directing soft money contributions to
these leadership PACs. These leadership PACs, moreover,
appear to constitute under the Act "entities" which are
"directly or indirectly established, financed, maintained or
controlled by" a federal officeholder or candidate. As such,
they are separately prohibited from solicitation, receipt,
direction, transfer or expenditure of these funds. In addition, the prohibition on the conduct of these activities by
an "agent" of candidates or officeholders would seem to
cover members of the leadership PAC staff, such as staff
raising funds.

These PACs may still, however, maintain federal and
nonfederal accounts, for use in federal and nonfederal
elections, respectively. The law's sponsors intended that
any amounts received for either type of account would
have to conform with federal law limits and source
restrictions. So a federal officeholder could raise $5,000
per calendar in "hard" money for the federal account
from a particular donor, and then raise, from that same

donor, another $5,000 for the nonfederal account regardless of whether state law would authorize larger individual contributions for state and local elections.[59] Stated differently, the federal limits apply in both instances, to both the federal and nonfederal monies raises from a particular contributor.

How these limits work may be illustrated by the example of contributions raised by a federal officeholder or candidate for a state party, rather than a "leadership PAC." The officeholder or candidate may raise from an individual $10,000 per calendar year for the party "hard" money account, and also the same amount for the party's nonfederal account. The federal limit applies in both instances. As noted previously, however, the federal officeholder or candidate may not raise any amount for a state party for use for certain "federal election activity" under the allowances of the Levin amendment.

Congressman Jones is approached by the state party of the state for fundraising support for state and local elections. Jones' state places no limit on corporate contributions to the party for those purposes. Jones, however, may only raise funds under federal limits for the party "nonfederal account": $10,000 from an individual per calendar year, and $5,000 per calendar year from a political committee.

Jones is also approached by a state political committee, not a unit of the state party, that supports candidates for state and local office who hold certain ambiguous and irrational positions. The state committee only functions on the state level: it does not make contributions to federal candidates. Jones may raise money for this state-level political committee, but only under federal limits: $5,000 per calendar year from either an individual or other political committee.

---

[59] Hence Senator McCain stated on the floor of the Senate:
A federal officeholder or candidate is prohibited from soliciting contributions for a Leadership PAC that do not comply with federal hard money source and amount limitations. Thus, the federal officeholder or candidate could solicit up to $5,000 per year from an individual or PAC for the federal account of the Leadership PAC and an additional $5,000 from an individual or PAC for the non-federal account of the Leadership PAC.

Jones, by now exhausted, is asked for assistance once more by the same state party seeking funds for Levin amendment get-out-the-vote activity. Jones may not raise funds for this purpose.

Raising money for state and local candidates

May a federal candidate or officeholder raise money for a state or local candidate, as when a member of the Congressional delegation solicits contributions for a candidate for Governor in her state, or when the Congresswoman who heads the ticket raises funds for candidates "down ballot"? She may, but only under federal law limits and source restrictions. Under this provision, federal campaign finance law supplants state law as it would otherwise apply to contributions raised for a state or local candidate. The federal candidate or officeholder may only raise $2,000 per election from an individual for any state or local candidate, and $5,000 a calendar year to that candidate from a PAC, even if state law were to provide for more generous limits for those candidates. Moreover, the Act's legislative history indicates that federal candidates or officeholders raising money from a single individual for state and local candidates must observe the aggregate limit on that individual's contributions. Specifically—

> A federal candidate or officeholder may not ask a single individual to donate amounts to all state candidates in a two-year election cycle that in the aggregate exceed $37,500, which corresponds to the aggregate amount of "hard money" that individuals may donate to all federal candidates over a two-year cycle.[60]

Regardless of the allowances of state law, the federal candidate or officeholder could not raise monies from corporations or unions for state and local candidates. These restrictions illustrate the determination of the drafters that federal candidates or officeholders not have anything to do with large or unlimited amounts of "soft money"—or perhaps more to the point, that donors have no more opportunity to buy favor with those

---

[60] *Id.*

candidates and officeholders by putting in their hands or at their disposal large sums of soft money.[61]

SUMMARY OF RESTRICTIONS ON FEDERAL CANDIDATE/OFFICEHOLDER FUNDRAISING

Generally:

1. May not "solicit, receive, direct, transfer," or spend soft money for any political organizations
   a. National parties;
   b. State and local parties [including for Levin Amendment activities];
   c. 527s;
   d. Leadership PACs or other multicandidate committees (but there is support in the legislative history for the proposition that officeholders may raise money separately for PAC "nonfederal accounts" under federal law limits)
2. Prohibition applies to:
   a. Their "agents";
   b. Entities they directly or indirectly establish finance, maintain, or control.

Examples:
   - "527s"
   - Leadership PACs

3. Exceptions:
   a. May solicit generally for a 501(c) charity if:
      i. Organization not engaged principally in certain election-related activities like voter registration; or
      ii. Organization principally engaged in these activities but officeholder or candidate only
      (a) Solicits individuals
      (b) Solicits from each individual no more than $20,000 in a calendar year
   b. Organization not engaged principally in certain election-related activities, but the

---

[61] Some federal officeholders may become candidates for state office, and the Act makes some allowance for them to raise and spend money for their own state and local purposes under the limits of state and local, rather than federal, law. The exception requires that the solicitation of the funds, and their later expenditure, refer "only to such state and local candidate" or her opponents for state or local office.

officeholder or candidate seeks to solicit funds specifically for those activities—and then may only solicit individuals for contributions of no more than $20,000 a calendar year.

c. May also run for a state office and solicit funds only for that office under state law

d. May "attend," speak, or be a featured guest at a state or local party "fundraising event"

The liability of federal candidates and officeholders

The provisions attaching personal liability to federal candidates and officeholders mark a sharp departure from the traditional approach of campaign finance laws. Those laws have generally operated to insulate candidates; who have been treated as "agents" of their own committees, and liability for illegal contributions received or expenditures made has typically fallen on those committees.

In broadly prohibiting "solicitations," the Act subjects federal candidates and officeholders to some uncertainty about the character of the offense they need to avoid. The term "solicitation" for purposes of this provision is not defined, but in another context—corporate solicitation of employees for PAC contributions—the FEC has defined it broadly. Under the broad definition, a "solicitation" can occur even if it is not explicit: it is enough for someone to discuss all the advantages or virtues of a contribution to a political committee, without actually asking that the contribution be made.

Thus, by this definition, an illegal solicitation could occur if a candidate or officeholder simply touts, to someone who later contributes, the strengths and past performance of a state party. As the FEC considers in the future what will be treated as a "solicitation" in enforcing the prohibition on candidate and officeholder solicitation, the legal risk that these candidates or officeholders run under this provision may become clearer.

Candidates, officeholders and criminal penalties for "knowing and willful" misconduct

In any event, the risks to the officeholder must be evaluated also in light of the sharply increased criminal exposure provided by the Act for "knowing and willful" violations. As discussed further below, the Act mandates the criminal enforcement of certain "knowing and willful" violations involving the "making, receiving, or reporting" of contributions or donations. The term "solicitation" does not appear in the language of this prohibition; but the act of solicitation is integrally related to the "making" of contributions. So it is possible that a candidate found to have solicited soft money "knowingly and willfully" would be subject to criminal penalties.

This concern with "solicitations" is not the only instance in the Act where it implicates the speech of the candidate or officeholder. It was noted earlier that the Act provides an exception from its broad prohibition on "soft money" fundraising for federal officeholders or candidates who "attend, speak, or [are]... featured guest[s] at a fundraising event for a state, district, or local committee of a political party." Nowhere in the existing law does there appear, as in the Act, any prohibition or explicit permission centered on candidate or officeholder speech. It would seem that, because the exception applies only to speech or attendance at state and local party fundraising event, the candidate or officeholder may not, for example, "speak" or appear as the featured guest at a "soft money" fundraising event of a state candidate, or of a multicandidate committee.

"You have permission to speak, Sir"

Restrictions on state and local candidates

State and local candidates are not home free under the Act. They, too, are subject to a prohibition on "soft money" fundraising, even if state law would otherwise permit it. A state candidate may not fund a "public communication" which in some way "refers" to a federal candidate, and also supports or opposes, or promotes or attacks, that candidate. A "public communication" includes the broadest range of communications, including broadcast, satellite and cablecast communications, as well as the use of mass mailings, phone banking, or any other form of "general public political advertising."[62] If the state candidate wishes to fund the communication, he must use only funds that meet federal law requirements for contributions—no union or corporate

---

[62] A mass mailing, as noted earlier, means more than 500 pieces of identical or substantially similar mail pieces sent out within a 30 day period, while a phone bank means more than 500 calls of an identical or substantially similar nature over a period of 30 days.

Limits, too, on state and local candidate "soft money"

general treasury, and no contributions from individuals that exceed $2,000 per election.

The concern of the Act is collusion between a state and federal candidate to funnel soft funds to the support of the federal candidate. An endorsement ad which refers to the federal candidate, such as by noting her support for the state and local candidate, but does not otherwise appear to support or promote the federal candidate, may be lawfully paid with soft money under state law.[63]

Governor James is running for another term on the same ticket with popular Senator Jones who is seeking reelection in the same year. Governor wishes to fund an ad through his gubernatorial committee featuring his relationship with Jones, and noting his share in major achievements by Jones in bringing development money to the state. James may not run this ad, unless his campaign pays for it with monies that meet federal limits and restrictions on source.

But state and local candidates are OK—if they keep quiet about federal candidates

The Act does allow the hapless James to run such an ad if it "is in connection with an election" for his state office—and refers "only" to him, or any other state and local candidate running for the same state and local office. This is a curious exception, seemingly premised on the mistaken belief that without it, there would be some question of whether an ad by a state candidate, mentioning only a state candidate, could be financed under state law. Federal law, however, could not purport to restrict the financing of such an ad in any event.

It will be a question, in any event, if federal law can prohibit the imagined ad featuring James alongside the popular Jones. James would be funding the ad for his own benefit, taking advantage of the high public approval of Jones. In this hypothetical, moreover, Jones realizes no personal gain from the ad: her personal ratings are high, and perhaps she is running without, or with only token, opposition. Yet the Act has laid down a highly prophylactic rule, one that focuses only

[63] 148 Cong. Rec. S2143 (daily ed. Mar. 20, 2002) (statement of Sen. Feingold).

on whether an ad "refers" to a federal candidate with apparent intention to favor or disfavor that candidate. If so, the other facts surrounding the communication make no difference. The state candidate may not fund the communication with state or "soft" funds.

Candidates' "personal use" of campaign funds

So much for federal candidates and officeholders and their "soft money." The Act makes some other adjustments in the federal law affecting federal candidates. It codifies much of the existing rulebook, developed by the FEC, defining and prohibiting candidates' "personal use" of their campaign funds. Existing law states only that "personal use" is prohibited, but the FEC has developed rules with considerably greater detail. The basic FEC scheme has been adopted in the Act, making these restrictions a matter of federal law—and emphasis—and not merely regulatory fiat. The Act states, as do the current FEC rules, that a candidate has made a prohibited "personal use" of her campaign funds if those funds are used to "fulfill any commitment, obligation, or expense of a person that would exist irrespective of the candidate's campaign...."[64]

"Personal use" of campaign funds

The Act reworks the regulatory language, and does not delve into qualifications and exceptions, though it is not clear that there is any intention to deprive the FEC of the continuing authority to provide for such qualifications and exceptions. Thus, for example, personal use under the Act includes payment of campaign funds for "a clothing purchase." The FEC rules set out the same prohibition, but with an exception for "items of *de minimis* value that are used in the campaign, such as campaign "T-shirts" or caps with campaign slogans. The Act's drafters were stressing that clothing could not be bought with campaign funds, but not expressing an objection to campaign T-shirts. The FEC rules will still govern the precise contours of each of the exceptions, and there also is a significant body of interpretations by the FEC over the years that still should be consulted.

---

[64] An officeholder may also use campaign funds to pay for certain expenses associated with his duties as a holder of federal office, subject to other statutory restrictions and rules of the House and Senate.

All the same, the Act stresses the key prohibitions, defining "personal use" to include
- Home mortgage, rent, or utility payment
- Clothing purchase
- Noncampaign-related automobile expense
- Country club membership
- Vacation or other noncampaign-related trip
- Household food item
- Tuition payment
- Admission to a sporting event, concert, theater, or other form of entertainment not associated with an election campaign
- Dues, fees, and other payments to a health club or recreational facility

What candidates may do with their campaign funds

At the same time, the Act identifies the exclusive uses to which campaign funds may be put. Other than expenditures "in connection with their campaigns," the Act leaves in place the allowance under existing law for the payment with campaign funds of ordinary and necessary expenses incurred in connection with the candidate's duties as "a holder of federal office." The officeholder considering payments for this purpose must, however, also consult the "ethics rules" of the House and Senate which control how officially related expenses are paid. The candidate may contribute with campaign funds to 501(c) charities, as recognized under the Internal Revenue Code, and she also may contribute without limitation from those funds to national, state, or local party committees.

CHAPTER 5

DISCLOSURE

The Act amends existing law to supplement and improve its various disclosure requirements. Previously noted has been the special disclosure of "electioneering communications"—ads by persons other than federal political committees that refer to a clearly identified federal candidate and are broadcast to the candidate's electorate within 30 days of a primary and 60 days of a general election. In addition, the Act promotes greater frequency of reporting by candidates and national party committees, and expands the range of reporting required of committees or individuals that make "independent expenditures." Another provision adds considerably to the requirement under existing law for "disclaimers" to be attached by political committees, candidates, and others to their general public political advertising for the purpose of disclosing the sponsorship of their ads. That provision also compels candidates and others who finance television and radio ads, including "negative ads," to include in those ads statements of responsibility or approval of their content. In support of these disclosure requirements, the Act mandates that the FEC direct the development of new reporting software, and also assure prompt distribution to the public via the Internet of reports filed with the FEC.

More frequent filings for national committees and candidates

The simplest provisions are those that mandate greater frequency of reporting by candidates and national party committees. Under existing law, candidates may elect in their off-years (years other than the year in which the election is scheduled) to file reports twice yearly of their receipts and disbursements. The Act eliminates this option, and imposes on them for those years—as well as for the actual election year—quarterly reporting. National party committees also are required to file monthly in place of quarterly reports.

Sponsorship identification—and candidate approval of ads

Existing law provides for certain disclosures—popularly referred to as "disclaimers"—that require "general public political advertising" to carry a statement of who paid for communications and whether a candidate authorized them. The Act adds to these requirements to assure the same disclosures for soft money activities, and also to compel the inclusion of statements of approval or responsibility by candidates or others who financed the ads. Certain of these requirements apply specifically to "negative" campaign ads.

Disclosing sponsorship of "soft money" communications

Political committees financing these ads with soft money—in whole or in part—must make a clear statement identifying who paid for and authorized them. A political committee is a committee registered with the FEC, but still able to spend "soft money" for some purposes. An example would be a state party, or a nonparty political committee, which unlike national party committees may maintain under the new law "soft money" accounts for some purposes. The Act provides that if such a political committee makes a soft money "disbursement" for "general public political advertising" allowed under the Act, the communications must carry the required statement of sponsorship. The same requirement holds for any "person" financing "electioneering communications," and in this instance, the Act also requires, in addition to disclosure of the person paying for the communication, additional information in the form of a "permanent street address, telephone number, or World Wide Web address."

Printed sponsorship notices

Printed "disclaimers" are subject under the Act to more exacting standards for presentation. The Act provides that these printed disclaimers

(1) be of sufficient type size to be clearly readable by the recipient of the communication;

(2) be contained in a printed box set apart from the other contents of the communication;

(3) be printed with a reasonable degree of color contrast between the background and the printed statement.

Candidates are subject under the Act to a new type of "disclaimers" for radio and television advertisements. Radio ads must carry "an audio statement by the candidate that identifies the candidate and states that the candidate has approved the communication." Television ads must also include such a statement, but the Act imposes some particular requirements, namely, that the statement:

(i)   shall be conveyed by

(I)   an unobscured, full-screen view of the candidate making the statement, or

(II)   the candidate in voice-over, accompanied by a clearly identifiable photographic or similar image of the candidate; and

(ii)   shall also appear in writing at the end of the communication in a clearly readable manner with a reasonable degree of color contrast between the background and the printed statement, for a period of at least 4 seconds. Statements by candidates and others of their "approval" of TV and radio statements

This requirement applies to persons other than candidates, including entities making "electioneering communications." The Act requires an audio statement about the political committee or other person paying for the ad, in the form of "[name of person] is responsible for the content of this advertising." The disclosure must also include the name of any "connected organization" of the payor. Thus, if the payor is a political committee of a trade association, for example, then the disclosure must include the name of the trade association, as well as its political committee. Television statements of approval are required of these organizations, as they are for candidate committees: a "representative" of the sponsoring organization must appear in an "unobscured, full-screen view," and the same statement must appear at the end in a writing with the requisite readability and reasonable color contrast.

Disclosure by "electioneering communications" and others

There will doubtless be some excitement in court about this requirement, inasmuch as the Act is mandating specific content in the ad—and in the case of the candidate, forcing her to *say something* in the ad. The drafters wished to enforce accountability for campaign statements, reflecting the view that campaign ads have taken a sad turn for the vicious and the viciously inac-

"Say it—or else"

curate. Should a candidate be required to take personal, even visual responsibility for ad content, it was assumed, she might consider more carefully what manner of tripe she cleared for broadcast. Whether this assumption holds also for outside groups making "electioneering communications," or PACs making independent expenditures, will be tested in time. Undue optimism should be held in check.

"Certifications" and disclaimers for "negative ads"

An additional control on content imposed by the Act on candidate ads takes aim at the "negative ad," the customary attack launched by one candidate at an opponent in paid advertising. The Act does not specifically refer to "negative" ads, but instead to ads in which the candidate makes a "direct reference to another candidate for the same office"; but the legislative history makes clear the intent.[65] Under the Act, candidates are not entitled to the benefits of the "lowest unit rate" under federal law for their purchase of broadcast time unless they certify to stations, in writing, that ads with this "direct reference" will carry certain statements of approval by the candidate. This requirement appears to overlap with the broad "disclaimer" requirement mentioned earlier, which also compels candidates to appear in those ads, by voice or image, to accept responsibility for them.

In the provision conditioning access to the lowest unit rate, the candidate must, in television ads, include in the ad, for a period of no less than 4 seconds,

(i)   a clearly identifiable photographic or similar image of the candidate; and

(ii)   a clearly readable printed statement, identifying the candidate and stating that the candidate has approved the broadcast and that the candidate's authorized committee paid for the broadcast.

A radio broadcast would include a "personal audio statement by the candidate" identifying herself, the office she seeks, and stating that she has approved the broadcast.

Should the candidate file a certification under this provision, but not meet these requirements in ads with

---

[65] The provision will "help slow the explosive growth of negative political commercials that are corroding the faith of individuals in the political process." 147 Cong. Rec. S2692 (daily ed. Mar. 22, 2001) (statement of Sen. Wyden).

a "direct reference" to another candidate, the candidate loses her entitlement to the "lowest unit rate" for all ads placed with the station within the periods before elections when the rates are in effect. Should the candidate decline to file the certification, then the candidate is also ineligible for the rate.

It is not clear how the statement required for an ad with a "direct reference" to another candidate would differ from, or be added in some way, to the statement of approval candidates are required to make in TV and radio broadcasts of any kind. The statements are different; but it would seem that the general one, applicable to all ads, would meet the requirements for the more specific one needed for a "direct reference" ad. Resolution of this question will be left to the FEC, but the courts will be asked first, most likely, to address the constitutionality of this content requirement as a condition of access to the lower unit rate.

The Act 's disclosure provisions also affect the reporting of independent expenditures, and expand the reporting requirement of those making them. Under existing law, the disclosure involves a statement of whether the expenditure supports or opposes the candidate, and under penalty of perjury, whether it was in fact made without the request or collaboration of the candidate. Contributors to the committee or person making the expenditure must be identified, if their contributions exceeded $200.00.

Independent expenditure reporting

These requirements are left in place, but the Act amends the existing requirement of a filing within 24 hours with the FEC of any independent expenditure aggregating $1,000 or more after the 20th day, but more than 24 hours, before the date of an election. The Act provides for additional reports, also filed within 24 hours, each time an additional expenditure of $1,000 or more is made. It also requires, as existing law does not, reports to be filed within 48 hours at any time up to the 20th day before an election, for any independent expenditure aggregating $10,000 more. Additional reports are required on a 48-hour basis for each additional aggregate expenditure of more than $10,000 in that election.

Access to broadcast stations for records of requests to buy political advertising

The Act promotes a different type of disclosure through an amendment to the Federal Communications Act, assuring public access to records of requests to broadcasters to purchase time for various kinds of political ads. These ads include those by or for candidates, but also by persons wishing to place ads on "a message relating to any political matter of national importance." Such messages are, for example, those popularly associated with "issue ads." They may refer to a candidate for public office, but they need not: the Act also secures access to records of requests for time for ads on "a national legislative issue of public importance."

The Act requires that broadcasters maintain records of these requests in some detail, including information on whether requests were rejected or accepted; the rate charged; the date and time of airing of the ads; and the name of the candidate or issue involved in the communication. The records must also contain, for ads other than those paid for by candidates, information about the person purchasing the time, including the name, address, and phone number of a contact person, along with a list of the chief executive officers or members of the executive committee or board of directors of the organization.

These requirements are intended to help trace the flow of "issue advertising" dollars. They apply to 527 or tax-exempt spending for election-related advertising, but do not depend on whether a candidate is named in the ad. Nor is there is any connection to periods immediately before elections: the access is guaranteed at all times, and the stations are required to maintain records for a period of not less than 2 years. With this information, the organizations engaged in advertising subject to these requirements must disclose their officers or representatives. The real "interests" behind such ads are, as a result, more readily identified.

Getting information, fast and on the web, through the FEC

The Act places new responsibilities under the FEC to assure improved, speedier public internet access to reports filed with the agency, and to develop special software that candidates would use to facilitate virtually instantaneous disclosure. The agency is mandated to make reports "accessible" to the public not later than

48 hours after receipt by the Commission, or within 24 hours if the report is one filed electronically. It must maintain a "central site" on the internet for public access to reports and other election-related information maintained by the Commission. Since the IRS receives the reports from "527s," it processes information that is "election-related," and the Act requires the two agencies, IRS and FEC, to coordinate toward making their reports available through or posted on the FEC site.

Reporting software for candidates – and instant reporting

The FEC is also mandated to promulgate standards for use by vendors in developing special reporting software. The software would be designed to more easily record information on receipts and disbursements while transmitting the recorded information immediately to the Commission and facilitating immediate internet posting by that agency. The FEC would provide the software, once available, to all candidates or committees filing under the Act. Candidates would be required to use this software for their reporting. The Act does not establish a timetable for the completion of this project. In light of the steps required—promulgation of standards and vendor development—some time may be required to bring it to fruition.

Inaugural committees

The Act also provides for one additional disclosure requirement, somewhat off the subject of campaign finance: donations to Presidential Inaugural Committees. For purpose of federal law, an "Inaugural Committee" is the committee appointed by the President-elect to "be in charge of the Presidential inaugural ceremony and functions and activities connected with the ceremony."[66] The Act conditions recognition of such a committee on its compliance with a requirement that it report donations of $200 or more to the Federal Election Commission within 90 days of the Inauguration. Beyond this reporting requirement, the Act prohibits acceptance by these committees of donations from foreign nationals.

[66] 36 U.S.C. § 501(1).

CHAPTER 6

ENFORCEMENT

The Act makes significant changes in the basic approach to enforcement of the federal campaign finance laws. It increases the penalties for some violations, changes the statute of limitations for criminal enforcement, and requires criminal sanctions in place of civil ones for certain "knowing and willful" violations.

Knowing and willful violations

Under existing law, the Act allows for two classes of civil violation. One, for want of better terms, is the garden-variety violation, while the other is one found to have been committed "knowingly and willfully." Under existing laws, knowing and willful violations are subject to heightened penalties; and they may also be referred to the Justice Department for criminal prosecution.[67]

The Act revises the approach to the treatment of "knowing and willful" penalties, apparently removing from the FEC the discretion to address civilly certain violations of that "knowing and willful" nature. Any person—candidate, committee, or other—who is found to have knowingly and willfully violated the law in "making, receiving, or reporting" any expenditure or donation aggregating $25,000 or more during a calendar year is subject to felony prosecution: either criminal fine, or imprisonment of not more than five years, or both fine and imprisonment. "Knowing and willful violations" aggregating at least $2,000 but less than $25,000 are also enforceable criminally, as misdemeanors, with fines, or imprisonment for not more than 1 year, or both.

Criminal penalties for "knowing and willful" violations

"Conduit" contributions

Another type of violation singled out for criminal enforcement is the prohibition on "conduit" contributions. Section 441 of the existing law provides:

---

[67] In some cases, the Department may elect against proceeding with prosecution in the first instance, and refer the matter to the FEC for consideration under a "knowing and willful" standard.

No person shall make a contribution in the name of another person or knowingly permit his name to be used to effect such a contribution and no person shall knowingly accept a contribution made by one person in the name of another person.

"Conduit" contributions: your name, my money

The conduct addressed in the provision takes the form of A, the true source of the funds, providing the money to B who then contributes the money in her own name. The making of conduit contributions came to widespread attention in enforcement actions arising out of the 1996 Presidential campaign. The Act reflects the intention to sharply increase the consequences for these violations.

Civil penalties for conduit violations

The Act raises the penalty level for "knowing and willful" violations of the "conduit" provision in two ways. First it increases the fines that may be imposed by the FEC—or by the courts upon suit by the FEC— for these kinds of violations. The violation is still "knowing and willful," but the penalty may be a civil one if the amount of money involved in the violation is less than $25,000. Under the existing law, a "knowing and willful" violation may be punished by a civil penalty not to exceed the greater of 1) $10,000, or 2) an amount equal to 200% of any contribution or expenditure involved in the violation. The Act raises these penalty levels for conduit contributions, to not less than 300% of the amount involved in the violation, and not more than the greater of 1) $50,000, or 2) 1,000% of the amount involved in the violation.

Criminal penalties for conduit violations

Second, the Act includes the application of criminal penalties for violations of this "conduit" prohibition aggregating more than $10,000 in a calendar year. The penalties include imprisonment, or a criminal fine, or both. The term of imprisonment is not to exceed two years; but it should be noted that if the amount involved is $25,000 or more, the term of imprisonment under the Act's general "knowing and willful" criminal penalty provisions could extend to five years. Alternatively, a criminal fine is mandated at the levels previously described for civil violations: not less than 300% of the amount involved in the violation, and not more than the greater of $50,000 or 1,000% of the amount involved in the violation.

Criminal sentencing standards

The commitment to increased criminal enforcement is also reflected in a mandate to the United States Sentencing Commission to promulgate or amend guidelines for criminal penalties for violations of the federal campaign finance laws, and to submit to Congress recommendations on improved enforcement. In developing its guidelines, which did not as of the passage of the Act specifically address violations of federal campaign finance laws, the Sentencing Commission is required to build into the guidelines certain "considerations"—including

> That the sentencing guidelines and policy statements reflect the serious nature of such violations and the need for aggressive and appropriate law enforcement action to prevent such violations.

Sentencing: campaign violations are serious

The Act also mandates the Commission to provide for "sentencing enhancement"—not a good thing—for certain kinds of violations. These are:

- foreign national contributions
- "a large number of illegal transactions"
- a "large aggregate amount" of illegal spending
- the receipt or disbursement of government funds
- "an intent to achieve a benefit from the federal government."

This last ground for sentencing enhancement is of some interest. By and large, the criminal laws have not focused successfully on whether a campaign contributor, in violating the Act, sought effectively an illicit advantage in influencing the official action of a candidate. It mattered only whether the law was violated; and the question of motivation was largely irrelevant. The consideration in sentencing of whether there was "an intent to achieve a benefit from the federal government" means that this issue of motivation has entered, in a sense, by the backdoor—not in the theory of prosecution, but in the determination of sentence in the event of a conviction.

A factor in sentencing: were you trying to buy something from the government?

Another similar question is raised by the consideration of whether the violation involved the receipt or disbursement of government funds. Existing law does not, by a specific exclusion, apply to the receipt or

Or were you using government property?

expenditure of federal government funds. For example, an officeholder who directs the use of government property to conduct campaign activity is violating other statutes and Congressional rules, but she is not committing a violation of the Federal Election Campaign Act. It is possible that the sentencing guideline mandate is intended to make this factor relevant by the "back door"—by making some use of government resources relevant to sentencing, even if it is not as a matter of law relevant to the theory of the prosecution or to the grounds for conviction.

Overall, the purpose of the amendment concerned with criminal penalties and enforcement is to encourage criminal prosecution of violations of the campaign finance laws. The existing law has been seen to have "structural flaws...that make it difficult for the more conscientious prosecutors to adequately pursue their cases"; the Act seeks to provide those prosecutors "with the tools they need to investigate and prosecute those who violate our campaign laws and attack the integrity of our electoral process." [68]

Statute of limitations

Existing law prohibits prosecution, trial or punishment for any criminal violation, "unless the indictment is found or the information is instituted within 3 years after the date of the violation." The Act extends this statute of limitations to 5 years, so that "prosecutors are [not] denied the time they need to pursue complex crimes."[69]

FEC rulemaking under the Act

Enforcement under the Act will also occur through rules promulgated by the FEC after enactment. The Act contemplates these rules, and mandates their completion within specified periods of time. The FEC is directed to promulgate rules on the provisions governing political parties within 90 days of enactment, and on all other provisions within nine months (270 days).

---

[68] 147 Cong. Rec. S3128 (daily ed. Mar. 29, 2001) (statement of Sen. Thompson).

[69] 147 Cong. Rec. S3128 (daily ed. March 29, 2001) (statement of Sen. Lieberman).

Nothing in the Act would prohibit those affected by the Act from initiating their own proposals for rule-making. It can be expected, in fact, that there will be such proposals to supplement whichever ones the FEC concludes that it should develop. Time works against the most comprehensive possible rulemaking effort: the 90-day period mandated by the Act includes the Commission's development of rules, its consideration of rulemaking proposals by others, opportunities for notice and comment, and then final rulemaking. It is likely that the 90-day rulemaking is the first in a series, and also that many persons will also choose to raise issues immediately for decision through requests for Advisory Opinions provided for by existing law.

A NOTE ON THE EFFECTIVE DATE FOR THE ACT—AND THE FRAMEWORK FOR LITIGATION

The Act takes effect generally on November 6, 2002. There are, however, some variations.

The party soft money provisions become effective on November 6, 2002, except that national party commit-tees may use soft money on hand as of that date through January 1, 2003, to retire debts and obliga-tions incurred solely in connection with the November general elections, or incurred after the date of those elections solely in connection with runoffs, recounts or election contests resulting from the November 2002 general elections. Those debts and obligations may be paid until 2003 with funds allocated between hard and soft accounts under the rules prescribed by the Federal Election Commission under existing law.

All the other provisions of the Act become effective November 6, 2002, with the exception of the modifica-tion in the "hard money" contribution limits. Increases in those limits are effective January 1, 2003.

In the meantime, litigation is in the offing,[70] and the

---

[70] Susan Milligan, "Campaign Finance Bill's Foes Initiate Legal Battle," *The Boston Globe*, Mar. 22, 2002 at A2; Frank J. Murray, "Finance reforms face test in court; Deciding issue to be free speech," *Washington Times*, Mar. 26, 2002 at A1.

Act defines the terms under which it will be conducted. An action challenging the constitutionality of any provision must be filed with a three-judge United States District Court for the District of Columbia. The final decision of that Court is appealable only to the Supreme Court of the United States, which must hear it. The timetable for consideration of these actions by both the District and Supreme Court is expedited by law. Each must advance the case on its docket, expediting "to the greatest possible extent" the disposition of the action. Members of Congress have the right to both challenge the Act directly, or to intervene on behalf of any party as a matter of right.

CONCLUSION

The Act represents a critical phase in the development of campaign finance controls in the United States. On this point, proponents and opponents of the reforms, as they prepare for court, can agree. Yet they agree for very different reasons, and these differences shed light on the large constitutional and regulatory questions presented by the Act.

Proponents are seeking to address what they perceive to be the collapse of earlier reforms—the erosion in the contribution limits and in the corporate and union spending prohibitions brought about by "soft money." They do not claim that theirs is a bold step, raising unprecedented constitutional issues, but rather that they are enforcing the existing scheme of limits and prohibitions upheld by the Supreme Court in *Buckley v. Valeo* a quarter of a century ago. If they are unable to do so, they will argue, Congress' will in enacting the existing law will be thwarted, and there can be no reasonable hope for serious campaign finance regulation in the United States. The steady increase in "soft money" fundraising and spending will continue, eventually overwhelming the existing law and rendering it, for all practical purposes, meaningless.

Opponents do not view the Act as a mechanism for enforcement of existing law, but as an extraordinary assertion of government control over free speech and association. Unlike existing law, dating back to the Federal Election Campaign Act amendments of 1974 and 1976, the Act reverses a longstanding presumption favoring political parties, and shaping to their advantage provisions of existing law. The "soft money" restrictions of the Act fall most broadly on the political parties, sharply limiting the resources available for advertising and voter registration and mobilization activities. By contrast, the 1974 amendments, concerned with preserving an enhanced role for parties, provided them with vastly more generous contribution limits than those available for other kinds of political committees. In addition, as opponents see it, the Act vitiates some of the key constitutional protections of *Buckley*, disregarding the stringent "express advocacy" test to impose on corporations and unions spending limitations and disclosure obligations affecting their use of "soft money" for "issue ads."

What accounts for these apparently irreconcilable perceptions—one that the Act is merely enforces the law as it exists, and the other that it is radical in its reach and threatening to constitutional values? The root of the conflict lies in the unresolved issue of how the seminal case of *Buckley* applied—or didn't—to government *enforcement* of statutory "loopholes". Under *Buckley*, this government concern with corruption, in appearance or fact, is the only permissible constitutional basis for government regulation; and any regulatory measure aimed at corruption may only pass constitutional muster if it is narrowly drawn to avoid unnecessary infringement of the rights of speech and association.[71] Yet as time passes and the government contends with "soft money" and other perceived "loopholes" and "circumventions," a key question is whether it must establish in each case that the challenged practice presents a direct threat of the fact or appearance or corruption—or whether the burden is lower, because the government is simply attempting to enforce existing law?

This is a question of large consequence in a political world of constantly changing and competitive fundraising and spending practices. The Supreme Court has yet to definitively answer that question. In an early case, the Court appeared to endorse the lower standard for enforcing existing law, holding that Congress could limit contributions to multicandidate committees—committees that, in turn, supported candidates—and not only contributions made directly to candidates. The Court held that this limit, one step removed from the candidates, was a "useful supplement" in "protecting the integrity of [the] legislative scheme." [72] Later Court cases went the other way, seeming to require that in seeking

---

[71] *Buckley*, 424 U.S. at 15. There is no dispute that these basic requirements of existing law are constitutional. Although some die-hard opponents of contribution limits look for opportunities to renew the attack on them, they have so far failed in their challenges to them. *Nixon v. Shrink Missouri Gov't PAC*, 528 U.S. 377 (2000).

[72] *California Medical Ass'n v. FEC*, 453 U.S. 182, 199 n.20 (1981); *see also FEC v. National Right to Work Comm.*, 459 U.S. 197 (1982).

to "plug" loopholes and enforce against unforeseen practices, the government was required to meet the stiff anti-corruption rationale of *Buckley*.[73]

The Act may well determine for some time to come which of these approaches will prevail in the review of the constitutionality of government enforcement efforts. In this respect, litigation over the Act will determine not only the fate of the new "soft money" restrictions, but also of future Congressional and regulatory efforts to uphold the *Buckley* scheme of contribution limitations and source restrictions. Proponents will argue that without some flexible constitutional authority to pursue enforcement, the Buckley world will collapse, as they perceive that it is doing under the weight of "soft money." But opponents will respond that if the "useful supplement" theory of enforcement is upheld, the government will have found a way around the constitutional "strict scrutiny" required of any regulatory controls on political finance. Opponents may fear that rather than accept that some reforms, like the contribution limits on individuals, will always be somewhat porous, the government will intensify its search for the cure, causing along the way considerable disruption to legitimate and necessary political activity.

There is always the possibility that the Court will appear to force a showing of compelling "anti-corruption" purpose, but still allow for a loose showing lacking in rigorous evidentiary standards. In that way, the Court could provide the government with what is effectively a lower standard, but without acknowledging that fact. It has seemed to do something like this in the past, in cases such as *Nixon*. There it found that the State of Missouri had made the requisite constitutional showing by submitting an affidavit from the co-chair of the legislature's Interim Joint Committee on Campaign Finance Reform, who simply declared that large contributions have "the real potential to buy votes."[74] It also accepted as evidence of the threat of these contributions, "newspaper accounts of large contributions supporting inferences of impropri-

---

[73] *FEC v. Massachusetts Citizens for Life*, 479 U.S. 238 (1986); *FEC v. National Conservative Political Action Comm. ("NCPAC")*, 470 U.S. 480 (1985).

[74] *Nixon*, 528 U.S. at 393.

ety." [75] Yet the Court reached the opposite conclusion about the value of newspaper accounts in *FEC v. NCPAC*.[76] The Congressional record of debate on the Act contains much material that, from the point of view of proponents of the reforms, is at least as potent as that which the Court considered in *Nixon*—and that from the point of view of opponents, is no more substantial or persuasive.

The Bipartisan Campaign Reform Act of 2002 is a defense of the reforms of the late 1970s, and the question before the Supreme Court, though phrased differently, will be how much room the Congress may claim to conduct that defense. The Act is complex, and some of its provisions are unprecedented. Among these provisions are the restrictions on fundraising and spending by political parties and their agents; on the political activities, including political speech, of federal candidates and officeholders; and on "outside group" advertising that addresses the conduct or votes of officeholders who also are candidates. The Act seeks to enforce these restrictions with more emphasis on criminal enforcement and heightened criminal penalties. Proponents may correctly believe that only this stiff dose of medication will cure the perceived ailments of existing law. Opponents will question, in turn, whether the patient will survive the treatment. The Supreme Court will eventually determine how much of the Act may be sustained in the name of upholding the original "Watergate" reforms of existing law.

Two additional issues may surface as the Act is brought before the Courts for review. One such issue is the independent significance, if any, of the right of association under the First Amendment. The Supreme Court has acknowledged that this right shares some billing with the right of speech, but it is a distinctly secondary billing. Under the analysis of the *Buckley* court, the significance of association is simply its enhancement of the right of speech. The *Buckley* emphasis on speech fit into the reform movement's political preoccupations at that time—a preoccupation with "fat cat" individual donors making large contributions to candidates, and to the political committees supporting candidates. The reform

---

[75] *Id.*

[76] 470 U.S. at 499.

effort has since shifted focus from restrictions on individuals to restrictions on political parties, and on "outside groups" vying with parties and candidates for advertising time and influence. In other words, attention has shifted to the activities of various kinds of associations. A striking manifestation of this shift is the *increase* the Act provides for individual contribution limits across-the-board, at the same time it sharply restricts the activities of parties and other groups. These developments may spur the Court to adjust its jurisprudence to more centrally consider the role of associative rights.

Another potential issue with practical impact, but without certain constitutional significance, is that of complexity. The existing law is complex as it stands, having expanded in the last 20 years in volume and intricacy as the FEC has issued advisory opinions and rules, and the courts have added their say through litigation. The Act adds considerably to that complexity. In some sense, this is an unavoidable development: as time passes, and candidates, parties, and others adjust to the law and changes in the political process with new practices raising new issues, the FEC attempts to adapt the law to new challenges.

Increased complexity does not assure improved enforcement. Instead, by producing some significant measure of confusion and raising the cost of compliance, complexity in the law raises the likelihood of mistakes resulting in violations. Courts may not have a precise doctrinal framework for capturing this concern with complexity, but it appears in some cases to have accounted for judicial resistance to FEC enforcement efforts under the existing law.[77] The Act's complexity, on its face and in possible application, also may weigh heavily on the pending constitutional review.

In the end, grave questions of public and private interest in America, including political questions, are inevitably framed and addressed as questions of law. Because the constitutional and legal questions embedded in the Act touch on the very conduct of political life, they are questions in which everyone—those who support the reforms and those who do not—has a profound stake.

---

[77] *See, e.g., FEC v. Harman*, 59 F. Supp. 2d (C.D. Cal. 1999).

APPENDIX
Bipartisan Campaign Reform Act of 2002

--H.R.2356--

H.R.2356

One Hundred Seventh Congress

of the

United States of America

AT THE SECOND SESSION

Begun and held at the City of Washington on Wednesday,

the twenty-third day of January, two thousand and two

An Act

To amend the Federal Election Campaign Act of 1971 to provide bipartisan campaign reform.

Be it enacted by the Senate and House of Representatives of the United States of America in Congress assembled,

SECTION 1. SHORT TITLE; TABLE OF CONTENTS.

(a) SHORT TITLE- This Act may be cited as the `Bipartisan Campaign Reform Act of 2002'.

(b) TABLE OF CONTENTS- The table of contents of this Act is as follows:

Sec. 315. Increase in penalties imposed for violations of conduit contribution ban.

Sec. 316. Restriction on increased contribution limits by taking into account candidate's available funds.

Sec. 317. Clarification of right of nationals of the United States to make political contributions.

Sec. 318. Prohibition of contributions by minors.

Sec. 319. Modification of individual contribution limits for House candidates in response to expenditures from personal funds.

TITLE IV--SEVERABILITY; EFFECTIVE DATE

Sec. 401. Severability.

Sec. 402. Effective dates and regulations.

Sec. 403. Judicial review.

TITLE V--ADDITIONAL DISCLOSURE PROVISIONS

Sec. 501. Internet access to records.

Sec. 502. Maintenance of website of election reports.

Sec. 503. Additional disclosure reports.

Sec. 504. Public access to broadcasting records.

TITLE I--REDUCTION OF SPECIAL INTEREST INFLUENCE

SEC. 101. SOFT MONEY OF POLITICAL PARTIES.

(a) IN GENERAL- Title III of the Federal Election Campaign Act of 1971 (2 U.S.C. 431 et seq.) is amended by adding at the end the following:

`SEC. 323. SOFT MONEY OF POLITICAL PARTIES.

`(a) NATIONAL COMMITTEES-

`(1) IN GENERAL- A national committee of a political party (including a national congressional campaign committee of a political party) may not solicit, receive, or direct to another person a contribution, donation, or transfer of funds or any other thing of value, or spend any funds, that are not subject to the limitations, prohibitions, and reporting requirements of this Act.

`(2) APPLICABILITY- The prohibition established by paragraph (1) applies to any such national committee, any officer or agent acting on behalf of such a national committee, and any entity that is directly or indirectly established, financed, maintained, or controlled by such a national committee.

`(b) STATE, DISTRICT, AND LOCAL COMMITTEES-

`(1) IN GENERAL- Except as provided in paragraph (2), an amount that is expended or disbursed for Federal election activity by a State, district, or local committee of a political party (including an entity that is directly or indirectly established, financed, maintained, or controlled by a State, district, or local committee of a political party and an officer or agent acting on behalf of such committee or entity), or by an association or similar group of candidates for State or local office or of individuals holding State or local office, shall be made from funds subject to the limitations, prohibitions, and reporting requirements of this Act.

`(2) APPLICABILITY-

`(A) IN GENERAL- Notwithstanding clause (i) or (ii) of section 301(20)(A), and subject to subparagraph (B), paragraph (1) shall not apply to any amount expended or disbursed by a State, district, or local committee of a political party for an activity described in either such clause to the extent the amounts expended or disbursed for such activity are allocated (under regulations prescribed by the Commission) among amounts--

`(i) which consist solely of contributions subject to the limitations, prohibitions, and reporting requirements of this Act (other than amounts described in subparagraph (B)(iii)); and

`(ii) other amounts which are not subject to the limitations, prohibitions, and reporting requirements of this Act (other than any requirements of this subsection).

`(B) CONDITIONS- Subparagraph (A) shall only apply if-

`(i) the activity does not refer to a clearly identified candidate for Federal office;

`(ii) the amounts expended or disbursed are not for the costs of any broadcasting, cable, or satellite communication, other than a communication which refers solely to a clearly identified candidate for State or local office;

-4-

`(iii) the amounts expended or disbursed which are described in subparagraph (A)(ii) are paid from amounts which are donated in accordance with State law and which meet the requirements of subparagraph (C), except that no person (including any person established, financed, maintained, or controlled by such person) may donate more than $10,000 to a State, district, or local committee of a political party in a calendar year for such expenditures or disbursements; and

`(iv) the amounts expended or disbursed are made solely from funds raised by the State, local, or district committee which makes such expenditure or disbursement, and do not include any funds provided to such committee from--

`(I) any other State, local, or district committee of any State party,

`(II) the national committee of a political party (including a national congressional campaign committee of a political party),

`(III) any officer or agent acting on behalf of any committee described in subclause (I) or (II), or

`(IV) any entity directly or indirectly established, financed, maintained, or controlled by any committee described in subclause (I) or (II).

`(C) PROHIBITING INVOLVEMENT OF NATIONAL PARTIES, FEDERAL CANDIDATES AND OFFICEHOLDERS, AND STATE PARTIES ACTING JOINTLY- Notwithstanding subsection (e) (other than subsection (e)(3)), amounts specifically authorized to be spent under subparagraph (B)(iii) meet the requirements of this subparagraph only if the amounts--

`(i) are not solicited, received, directed, transferred, or spent by or in the name of any person described in subsection (a) or (e); and

`(ii) are not solicited, received, or directed through fundraising activities conducted jointly by 2 or more State, local, or district committees of any political party or their agents, or by a State, local, or district committee of a political party on behalf of the State, local, or district committee of a political party or its agent in one or more other States.

`(c) FUNDRAISING COSTS- An amount spent by a person described in subsection (a) or (b) to raise funds that are used, in whole or in part, for expenditures and disbursements for a Federal election activity shall be made from funds subject to the limitations, prohibitions, and reporting requirements of this Act.

`(d) TAX-EXEMPT ORGANIZATIONS- A national, State, district, or local committee of a political party (including a national congressional campaign committee of a political party), an entity that is directly or indirectly established, financed, maintained, or controlled by any such national, State, district, or local committee or its agent, and an officer or agent acting on behalf of any such party committee or entity, shall not solicit any funds for, or make or direct any donations to--

`(1) an organization that is described in section 501(c) of the Internal Revenue Code of 1986 and exempt from taxation under section 501(a) of such Code (or has submitted an application for determination of tax exempt status under such section) and that makes expenditures or disbursements in connection with an election for Federal office (including expenditures or disbursements for Federal election activity); or

`(2) an organization described in section 527 of such Code (other than a political committee, a State, district, or local committee of a political party, or the authorized campaign committee of a candidate for State or local office).

`(e) FEDERAL CANDIDATES-

`(1) IN GENERAL- A candidate, individual holding Federal office, agent of a candidate or an individual holding Federal office, or an entity directly or indirectly established, financed, maintained or controlled by or acting on behalf of 1 or more candidates or individuals holding Federal office, shall not--

`(A) solicit, receive, direct, transfer, or spend funds in connection with an election for Federal office, including funds for any Federal election activity, unless the funds are subject to the limitations, prohibitions, and reporting requirements of this Act; or

`(B) solicit, receive, direct, transfer, or spend funds in connection with any election other than an election for Federal office or disburse funds in connection with such an election unless the funds-

`(i) are not in excess of the amounts permitted with respect to contributions to candidates and political committees under paragraphs (1), (2), and (3) of section 315(a); and `(ii) are not from sources prohibited by this Act from making contributions in connection with an election for Federal office.

`(2) STATE LAW- Paragraph (1) does not apply to the solicitation, receipt, or spending of funds by an individual described in such paragraph who is or was also a candidate for a State or local office solely in connection with such election for State or local office if the solicitation, receipt, or spending of funds is permitted under State law and refers only to such State or local candidate, or to any other candidate for the State or local office sought by such candidate, or both.

`(3) FUNDRAISING EVENTS- Notwithstanding paragraph (1) or subsection (b)(2)(C), a candidate or an individual holding Federal office may attend, speak, or be a featured guest at a fundraising event for a State, district, or local committee of a political party.

`(4) PERMITTING CERTAIN SOLICITATIONS-

`(A) GENERAL SOLICITATIONS- Notwithstanding any other provision of this subsection, an individual described in paragraph (1) may make a general solicitation of funds on behalf of any organization that is described in section 501(c) of the Internal Revenue Code of 1986 and exempt from taxation under section 501(a) of such Code (or has submitted an application for determination of tax exempt status under such section) (other than an entity whose principal purpose is to conduct activities described in clauses (i) and (ii) of section 301(20)(A)) where such solicitation does not specify how the funds will or should be spent.

`(B) CERTAIN SPECIFIC SOLICITATIONS- In addition to the general solicitations permitted under subparagraph (A), an individual described in paragraph (1) may make a solicitation explicitly to obtain funds for carrying out the activities described in clauses (i) and (ii) of section 301(20)(A), or for an entity whose principal purpose is to conduct such activities, if--

`(i) the solicitation is made only to individuals; and

`(ii) the amount solicited from any individual during any calendar year does not exceed $20,000.

`(f) STATE CANDIDATES-

`(1) IN GENERAL- A candidate for State or local office, individual holding State or local office, or an agent of such a candidate or individual may not spend any funds for a communication described in section 301(20)(A)(iii) unless the funds are subject to the limitations, prohibitions, and reporting requirements of this Act.

`(2) EXCEPTION FOR CERTAIN COMMUNICATIONS- Paragraph (1) shall not apply to an individual described in such paragraph if the communication involved is in connection with an election for such State or local office and refers only to such individual or to any other candidate for the State or local office held or sought by such individual, or both.'.

(b) DEFINITIONS- Section 301 of the Federal Election Campaign Act of 1971 (2 U.S.C. 431) is amended by adding at the end thereof the following:

`(20) FEDERAL ELECTION ACTIVITY-

`(A) IN GENERAL- The term `Federal election activity' means-

`(i) voter registration activity during the period that begins on the date that is 120 days before the date a regularly scheduled Federal election is held and ends on the date of the election;

`(ii) voter identification, get-out-the-vote activity, or generic campaign activity conducted in connection with an election in which a candidate for Federal office appears on the ballot (regardless of whether a candidate for State or local office also appears on the ballot);

`(iii) a public communication that refers to a clearly identified candidate for Federal office (regardless of whether a candidate for State or local office is also mentioned or identified) and that promotes or supports a candidate for that office, or attacks or opposes a candidate for that office (regardless of whether the communication expressly advocates a vote for or against a candidate); or

`(iv) services provided during any month by an employee of a State, district, or local committee of a political party who spends more than 25 percent of that individual's compensated time during that month on activities in connection with a Federal election.

`(B) EXCLUDED ACTIVITY- The term `Federal election activity' does not include an amount expended or disbursed by a State, district, or local committee of a political party for--

-8-

`(i) a public communication that refers solely to a clearly identified candidate for State or local office, if the communication is not a Federal election activity described in subparagraph (A)(i) or (ii);

`(ii) a contribution to a candidate for State or local office, provided the contribution is not designated to pay for a Federal election activity described in subparagraph (A);

`(iii) the costs of a State, district, or local political convention; and

`(iv) the costs of grassroots campaign materials, including buttons, bumper stickers, and yard signs, that name or depict only a candidate for State or local office.

`(21) GENERIC CAMPAIGN ACTIVITY- The term `generic campaign activity' means a campaign activity that promotes a political party and does not promote a candidate or non-Federal candidate.

`(22) PUBLIC COMMUNICATION- The term `public communication' means a communication by means of any broadcast, cable, or satellite communication, newspaper, magazine, outdoor advertising facility, mass mailing, or telephone bank to the general public, or any other form of general public political advertising.

`(23) MASS MAILING- The term `mass mailing' means a mailing by United States mail or facsimile of more than 500 pieces of mail matter of an identical or substantially similar nature within any 30-day period.

`(24) TELEPHONE BANK- The term `telephone bank' means more than 500 telephone calls of an identical or substantially similar nature within any 30-day period.'.

SEC. 102. INCREASED CONTRIBUTION LIMIT FOR STATE COMMITTEES OF POLITICAL PARTIES.

Section 315(a)(1) of the Federal Election Campaign Act of 1971 (2 U.S.C. 441a(a)(1)) is amended--

(1) in subparagraph (B), by striking `or' at the end;

(2) in subparagraph (C)--

(A) by inserting `(other than a committee described in subparagraph (D))' after `committee'; and

APPENDIX | 117

(B) by striking the period at the end and inserting `; or'; and

(3) by adding at the end the following:

`(D) to a political committee established and maintained by a State committee of a political party in any calendar year which, in the aggregate, exceed $10,000.'.

SEC. 103. REPORTING REQUIREMENTS.

(a) REPORTING REQUIREMENTS- Section 304 of the Federal Election Campaign Act of 1971 (2 U.S.C. 434) is amended by adding at the end the following:

`(e) POLITICAL COMMITTEES-

`(1) NATIONAL AND CONGRESSIONAL POLITICAL COMMITTEES- The national committee of a political party, any national congressional campaign committee of a political party, and any subordinate committee of either, shall report all receipts and disbursements during the reporting period.

`(2) OTHER POLITICAL COMMITTEES TO WHICH SECTION 323 APPLIES-

`(A) IN GENERAL- In addition to any other reporting requirements applicable under this Act, a political committee (not described in paragraph (1)) to which section 323(b)(1) applies shall report all receipts and disbursements made for activities described in section 301(20)(A), unless the aggregate amount of such receipts and disbursements during the calendar year is less than $5,000.

`(B) SPECIFIC DISCLOSURE BY STATE AND LOCAL PARTIES OF CERTAIN NON-FEDERAL AMOUNTS PERMITTED TO BE SPENT ON FEDERAL ELECTION ACTIVITY- Each report by a political committee under subparagraph (A) of receipts and disbursements made for activities described in section 301(20)(A) shall include a disclosure of all receipts and disbursements described in section 323(b)(2)(A) and (B).

`(3) ITEMIZATION- If a political committee has receipts or disbursements to which this subsection applies from or to any person aggregating in excess of $200 for any calendar year, the political committee shall separately itemize its reporting for such person in the same manner as required in paragraphs (3)(A), (5), and (6) of subsection (b).

-10-

`(4) REPORTING PERIODS- Reports required to be filed under this subsection shall be filed for the same time periods required for political committees under subsection (a)(4)(B).'.

(b) BUILDING FUND EXCEPTION TO THE DEFINITION OF CONTRIBUTION-

(1) IN GENERAL- Section 301(8)(B) of the Federal Election Campaign Act of 1971 (2 U.S.C. 431(8)(B)) is amended--

(A) by striking clause (viii); and

(B) by redesignating clauses (ix) through (xv) as clauses (viii) through (xiv), respectively.

(2) NONPREEMPTION OF STATE LAW- Section 403 of such Act (2 U.S.C. 453) is amended--

(A) by striking `The provisions of this Act' and inserting `(a) IN GENERAL- Subject to subsection (b), the provisions of this Act'; and

(B) by adding at the end the following:

`(b) STATE AND LOCAL COMMITTEES OF POLITICAL PARTIES- Notwithstanding any other provision of this Act, a State or local committee of a political party may, subject to State law, use exclusively funds that are not subject to the prohibitions, limitations, and reporting requirements of the Act for the purchase or construction of an office building for such State or local committee.'.

TITLE II--NONCANDIDATE CAMPAIGN EXPENDITURES

Subtitle A--Electioneering Communications

SEC. 201. DISCLOSURE OF ELECTIONEERING COMMUNICATIONS.

(a) IN GENERAL- Section 304 of the Federal Election Campaign Act of 1971 (2 U.S.C. 434), as amended by section 103, is amended by adding at the end the following new subsection:

`(f) DISCLOSURE OF ELECTIONEERING COMMUNICATIONS-

`(1) STATEMENT REQUIRED- Every person who makes a disbursement for the direct costs of producing and airing electioneering communications in an aggregate amount in excess of $10,000 during any calendar year shall, within 24 hours of each disclosure date, file with the Commission a statement containing the information described in paragraph (2).

`(2) CONTENTS OF STATEMENT- Each statement required to be filed under this subsection shall be made under penalty of perjury and shall contain the following information:

`(A) The identification of the person making the disbursement, of any person sharing or exercising direction or control over the activities of such person, and of the custodian of the books and accounts of the person making the disbursement.

`(B) The principal place of business of the person making the disbursement, if not an individual.

`(C) The amount of each disbursement of more than $200 during the period covered by the statement and the identification of the person to whom the disbursement was made.

`(D) The elections to which the electioneering communications pertain and the names (if known) of the candidates identified or to be identified.

`(E) If the disbursements were paid out of a segregated bank account which consists of funds contributed solely by individuals who are United States citizens or nationals or lawfully admitted for permanent residence (as defined in section 101(a)(20) of the Immigration and Nationality Act (8 U.S.C. 1101(a)(20))) directly to this account for electioneering communications, the names and addresses of all contributors who contributed an aggregate amount of $1,000 or more to that account during the period beginning on the first day of the preceding calendar year and ending on the disclosure date. Nothing in this subparagraph is to be construed as a prohibition on the use of funds in such a segregated account for a purpose other than electioneering communications.

`(F) If the disbursements were paid out of funds not described in subparagraph (E), the names and addresses of all contributors who contributed an aggregate amount of $1,000 or more to the person making the disbursement during the period beginning on the first day of the preceding calendar year and ending on the disclosure date.

`(3) ELECTIONEERING COMMUNICATION- For purposes of this subsection--

`(A) IN GENERAL- (i) The term `electioneering communication' means any broadcast, cable, or satellite communication which--

-12-

`(I) refers to a clearly identified candidate for Federal office;

`(II) is made within--

`(aa) 60 days before a general, special, or runoff election for the office sought by the candidate; or

`(bb) 30 days before a primary or preference election, or a convention or caucus of a political party that has authority to nominate a candidate, for the office sought by the candidate; and

`(III) in the case of a communication which refers to a candidate for an office other than President or Vice President, is targeted to the relevant electorate.

`(ii) If clause (i) is held to be constitutionally insufficient by final judicial decision to support the regulation provided herein, then the term `electioneering communication' means any broadcast, cable, or satellite communication which promotes or supports a candidate for that office, or attacks or opposes a candidate for that office (regardless of whether the communication expressly advocates a vote for or against a candidate) and which also is suggestive of no plausible meaning other than an exhortation to vote for or against a specific candidate. Nothing in this subparagraph shall be construed to affect the interpretation or application of section 100.22(b) of title 11, Code of Federal Regulations.

`(B) EXCEPTIONS- The term `electioneering communication' does not include--

`(i) a communication appearing in a news story, commentary, or editorial distributed through the facilities of any broadcasting station, unless such facilities are owned or controlled by any political party, political committee, or candidate;

`(ii) a communication which constitutes an expenditure or an independent expenditure under this Act;

`(iii) a communication which constitutes a candidate debate or forum conducted pursuant to regulations adopted by the Commission, or which solely promotes such a debate or forum and is made by or on behalf of the person sponsoring the debate or forum; or `(iv) any other communication exempted under such regulations as the Commission may promulgate (consistent with the requirements of this paragraph) to ensure the appropriate implementation of this paragraph, except that under any such regulation a communication may not be exempted if it meets the requirements of this paragraph and is described in section 301(20)(A)(iii).

`(C) TARGETING TO RELEVANT ELECTORATE- For purposes of this paragraph, a communication which refers to a clearly identified candidate for Federal office is `targeted to the relevant electorate' if the communication can be received by 50,000 or more persons--

`(i) in the district the candidate seeks to represent, in the case of a candidate for Representative in, or Delegate or Resident Commissioner to, the Congress; or

`(ii) in the State the candidate seeks to represent, in the case of a candidate for Senator.

`(4) DISCLOSURE DATE- For purposes of this subsection, the term `disclosure date' means--

`(A) the first date during any calendar year by which a person has made disbursements for the direct costs of producing or airing electioneering communications aggregating in excess of $10,000; and

`(B) any other date during such calendar year by which a person has made disbursements for the direct costs of producing or airing electioneering communications aggregating in excess of $10,000 since the most recent disclosure date for such calendar year.

`(5) CONTRACTS TO DISBURSE- For purposes of this subsection, a person shall be treated as having made a disbursement if the person has executed a contract to make the disbursement.

`(6) COORDINATION WITH OTHER REQUIREMENTS- Any requirement to report under this subsection shall be in addition to any other reporting requirement under this Act.

`(7) COORDINATION WITH INTERNAL REVENUE CODE- Nothing in this subsection may be construed to establish, modify, or otherwise affect the definition of political activities or electioneering activities (including the definition of participating in, intervening in, or influencing or attempting to influence a political campaign on behalf of or in opposition to

-14-

any candidate for public office) for purposes of the Internal Revenue Code of 1986.'.

(b) RESPONSIBILITIES OF FEDERAL COMMUNICATIONS COMMISSION- The Federal Communications Commission shall compile and maintain any information the Federal Election Commission may require to carry out section 304(f) of the Federal Election Campaign Act of 1971 (as added by subsection (a)), and shall make such information available to the public on the Federal Communication Commission's website.

SEC. 202. COORDINATED COMMUNICATIONS AS CONTRIBUTIONS.

Section 315(a)(7) of the Federal Election Campaign Act of 1971 (2 U.S.C. 441a(a)(7)) is amended--

(1) by redesignating subparagraph (C) as subparagraph (D); and

(2) by inserting after subparagraph (B) the following:

`(C) if--

`(i) any person makes, or contracts to make, any disbursement for any electioneering communication (within the meaning of section 304(f)(3)); and

`(ii) such disbursement is coordinated with a candidate or an authorized committee of such candidate, a Federal, State, or local political party or committee thereof, or an agent or official of any such candidate, party, or committee;

such disbursement or contracting shall be treated as a contribution to the candidate supported by the electioneering communication or that candidate's party and as an expenditure by that candidate or that candidate's party; and'.

SEC. 203. PROHIBITION OF CORPORATE AND LABOR DISBURSEMENTS FOR ELECTIONEERING COMMUNICATIONS.

(a) IN GENERAL- Section 316(b)(2) of the Federal Election Campaign Act of 1971 (2 U.S.C. 441b(b)(2)) is amended by inserting `or for any applicable electioneering communication' before `, but shall not include'.

(b) APPLICABLE ELECTIONEERING COMMUNICATION- Section 316 of such Act is amended by adding at the end the following:

`(c) RULES RELATING TO ELECTIONEERING COMMUNICATIONS-

-15-

'(1) APPLICABLE ELECTIONEERING COMMUNICATION- For purposes of this section, the term 'applicable electioneering communication' means an electioneering communication (within the meaning of section 304(f)(3)) which is made by any entity described in subsection (a) of this section or by any other person using funds donated by an entity described in subsection (a) of this section.

'(2) EXCEPTION- Notwithstanding paragraph (1), the term 'applicable electioneering communication' does not include a communication by a section 501(c)(4) organization or a political organization (as defined in section 527(e)(1) of the Internal Revenue Code of 1986) made under section 304(f)(2)(E) or (F) of this Act if the communication is paid for exclusively by funds provided directly by individuals who are United States citizens or nationals or lawfully admitted for permanent residence (as defined in section 101(a)(20) of the Immigration and Nationality Act (8 U.S.C. 1101(a)(20))). For purposes of the preceding sentence, the term 'provided directly by individuals' does not include funds the source of which is an entity described in subsection (a) of this section.

'(3) SPECIAL OPERATING RULES-

'(A) DEFINITION UNDER PARAGRAPH (1)- An electioneering communication shall be treated as made by an entity described in subsection (a) if an entity described in subsection (a) directly or indirectly disburses any amount for any of the costs of the communication.

'(B) EXCEPTION UNDER PARAGRAPH (2)- A section 501(c)(4) organization that derives amounts from business activities or receives funds from any entity described in subsection (a) shall be considered to have paid for any communication out of such amounts unless such organization paid for the communication out of a segregated account to which only individuals can contribute, as described in section 304(f)(2)(E).

'(4) DEFINITIONS AND RULES- For purposes of this subsection--

'(A) the term 'section 501(c)(4) organization' means--

'(i) an organization described in section 501(c)(4) of the Internal Revenue Code of 1986 and exempt from taxation under section 501(a) of such Code; or

'(ii) an organization which has submitted an application to the Internal Revenue Service for determination of its status as an organization described in clause (i); and

`(B) a person shall be treated as having made a disbursement if the person has executed a contract to make the disbursement.

`(5) COORDINATION WITH INTERNAL REVENUE CODE- Nothing in this subsection shall be construed to authorize an organization exempt from taxation under section 501(a) of the Internal Revenue Code of 1986 to carry out any activity which is prohibited under such Code.'.

SEC. 204. RULES RELATING TO CERTAIN TARGETED ELECTIONEERING COMMUNICATIONS.

Section 316(c) of the Federal Election Campaign Act of 1971 (2 U.S.C. 441b), as added by section 203, is amended by adding at the end the following:

`(6) SPECIAL RULES FOR TARGETED COMMUNICATIONS-

`(A) EXCEPTION DOES NOT APPLY- Paragraph (2) shall not apply in the case of a targeted communication that is made by an organization described in such paragraph.

`(B) TARGETED COMMUNICATION- For purposes of subparagraph (A), the term `targeted communication' means an electioneering communication (as defined in section 304(f)(3)) that is distributed from a television or radio broadcast station or provider of cable or satellite television service and, in the case of a communication which refers to a candidate for an office other than President or Vice President, is targeted to the relevant electorate.

`(C) DEFINITION- For purposes of this paragraph, a communication is `targeted to the relevant electorate' if it meets the requirements described in section 304(f)(3)(C).'.

Subtitle B--Independent and Coordinated Expenditures

SEC. 211. DEFINITION OF INDEPENDENT EXPENDITURE.

Section 301 of the Federal Election Campaign Act (2 U.S.C. 431) is amended by striking paragraph (17) and inserting the following:

`(17) INDEPENDENT EXPENDITURE- The term `independent expenditure' means an expenditure by a person--

`(A) expressly advocating the election or defeat of a clearly identified candidate; and

`(B) that is not made in concert or cooperation with or at the request or suggestion of such candidate, the candidate's authorized

political committee, or their agents, or a political party committee or
its agents.'.

SEC. 212. REPORTING REQUIREMENTS FOR CERTAIN INDEPENDENT EXPENDITURES.

(a) IN GENERAL- Section 304 of the Federal Election Campaign Act of 1971
(2 U.S.C. 434) (as amended by section 201) is amended--

(1) in subsection (c)(2), by striking the undesignated matter after
subparagraph (C); and

(2) by adding at the end the following:

'(g) TIME FOR REPORTING CERTAIN EXPENDITURES-

'(1) EXPENDITURES AGGREGATING $1,000-

'(A) INITIAL REPORT- A person (including a political
committee) that makes or contracts to make independent expenditures
aggregating $1,000 or more after the 20th day, but more than 24 hours,
before the date of an election shall file a report describing the
expenditures within 24 hours.

'(B) ADDITIONAL REPORTS- After a person files a report
under subparagraph (A), the person shall file an additional report
within 24 hours after each time the person makes or contracts to make
independent expenditures aggregating an additional $1,000 with
respect to the same election as that to which the initial report relates.

'(2) EXPENDITURES AGGREGATING $10,000-

'(A) INITIAL REPORT- A person (including a political
committee) that makes or contracts to make independent expenditures
aggregating $10,000 or more at any time up to and including the 20th
day before the date of an election shall file a report describing the
expenditures within 48 hours.

'(B) ADDITIONAL REPORTS- After a person files a report
under subparagraph (A), the person shall file an additional report
within 48 hours after each time the person makes or contracts to make
independent expenditures aggregating an additional $10,000 with
respect to the same election as that to which the initial report relates.

'(3) PLACE OF FILING; CONTENTS- A report under this
subsection--

'(A) shall be filed with the Commission; and

'(B) shall contain the information required by subsection (b)(6)(B)(iii), including the name of each candidate whom an expenditure is intended to support or oppose.'.

(b) TIME OF FILING OF CERTAIN STATEMENTS-

(1) IN GENERAL- Section 304(g) of such Act, as added by subsection (a), is amended by adding at the end the following:

'(4) TIME OF FILING FOR EXPENDITURES AGGREGATING $1,000- Notwithstanding subsection (a)(5), the time at which the statement under paragraph (1) is received by the Commission or any other recipient to whom the notification is required to be sent shall be considered the time of filing of the statement with the recipient.'.

(2) CONFORMING AMENDMENTS- (A) Section 304(a)(5) of such Act (2 U.S.C. 434(a)(5)) is amended by striking 'the second sentence of subsection (c)(2)' and inserting 'subsection (g)(1)'.

(B) Section 304(d)(1) of such Act (2 U.S.C. 434(d)(1)) is amended by inserting 'or (g)' after 'subsection (c)'.

SEC. 213. INDEPENDENT VERSUS COORDINATED EXPENDITURES BY PARTY.

Section 315(d) of the Federal Election Campaign Act of 1971 (2 U.S.C. 441a(d)) is amended--

(1) in paragraph (1), by striking 'and (3)' and inserting ', (3), and (4)'; and

(2) by adding at the end the following:

'(4) INDEPENDENT VERSUS COORDINATED EXPENDITURES BY PARTY-

'(A) IN GENERAL- On or after the date on which a political party nominates a candidate, no committee of the political party may make--

'(i) any coordinated expenditure under this subsection with respect to the candidate during the election cycle at any time after it makes any independent expenditure (as defined in section 301(17)) with respect to the candidate during the election cycle; or `(ii) any independent expenditure (as defined in section 301(17)) with respect to the candidate during the election cycle at any time after it makes any coordinated expenditure under this subsection with respect to the candidate during the election cycle.

`(B) APPLICATION- For purposes of this paragraph, all political committees established and maintained by a national political party (including all congressional campaign committees) and all political committees established and maintained by a State political party (including any subordinate committee of a State committee) shall be considered to be a single political committee.

`(C) TRANSFERS- A committee of a political party that makes coordinated expenditures under this subsection with respect to a candidate shall not, during an election cycle, transfer any funds to, assign authority to make coordinated expenditures under this subsection to, or receive a transfer of funds from, a committee of the political party that has made or intends to make an independent expenditure with respect to the candidate.'.

SEC. 214. COORDINATION WITH CANDIDATES OR POLITICAL PARTIES.

(a) IN GENERAL- Section 315(a)(7)(B) of the Federal Election Campaign Act of 1971 (2 U.S.C. 441a(a)(7)(B)) is amended--

(1) by redesignating clause (ii) as clause (iii); and

(2) by inserting after clause (i) the following new clause:

`(ii) expenditures made by any person (other than a candidate or candidate's authorized committee) in cooperation, consultation, or concert with, or at the request or suggestion of, a national, State, or local committee of a political party, shall be considered to be contributions made to such party committee; and'.

(b) REPEAL OF CURRENT REGULATIONS- The regulations on coordinated communications paid for by persons other than candidates, authorized committees of candidates, and party committees adopted by the Federal Election Commission and published in the Federal Register at page 76138 of volume 65, Federal Register, on December 6, 2000, are repealed as of the date by which the Commission is required to promulgate new regulations under subsection (c) (as described in section 402(c)(1)).

(c) REGULATIONS BY THE FEDERAL ELECTION COMMISSION- The Federal Election Commission shall promulgate new regulations on coordinated communications paid for by persons other than candidates, authorized committees of candidates, and party committees. The regulations shall not require agreement or formal collaboration to establish coordination. In addition to any subject determined by the Commission, the regulations shall address--

(1) payments for the republication of campaign materials;

(2) payments for the use of a common vendor;

(3) payments for communications directed or made by persons who previously served as an employee of a candidate or a political party; and

(4) payments for communications made by a person after substantial discussion about the communication with a candidate or a political party.

(d) MEANING OF CONTRIBUTION OR EXPENDITURE FOR THE PURPOSES OF SECTION 316- Section 316(b)(2) of the Federal Election Campaign Act of 1971 (2 U.S.C. 441b(b)(2)) is amended by striking `shall include' and inserting `includes a contribution or expenditure, as those terms are defined in section 301, and also includes'.

TITLE III--MISCELLANEOUS

SEC. 301. USE OF CONTRIBUTED AMOUNTS FOR CERTAIN PURPOSES.

Title III of the Federal Election Campaign Act of 1971 (2 U.S.C. 431 et seq.) is amended by striking section 313 and inserting the following:

`SEC. 313. USE OF CONTRIBUTED AMOUNTS FOR CERTAIN PURPOSES.

`(a) PERMITTED USES- A contribution accepted by a candidate, and any other donation received by an individual as support for activities of the individual as a holder of Federal office, may be used by the candidate or individual--

`(1) for otherwise authorized expenditures in connection with the campaign for Federal office of the candidate or individual;

`(2) for ordinary and necessary expenses incurred in connection with duties of the individual as a holder of Federal office;

`(3) for contributions to an organization described in section 170(c) of the Internal Revenue Code of 1986; or

`(4) for transfers, without limitation, to a national, State, or local committee of a political party.

`(b) PROHIBITED USE-

`(1) IN GENERAL- A contribution or donation described in subsection (a) shall not be converted by any person to personal use.

'(2) CONVERSION- For the purposes of paragraph (1), a contribution or donation shall be considered to be converted to personal use if the contribution or amount is used to fulfill any commitment, obligation, or expense of a person that would exist irrespective of the candidate's election campaign or individual's duties as a holder of Federal office, including--

'(A) a home mortgage, rent, or utility payment;

'(B) a clothing purchase;

'(C) a noncampaign-related automobile expense;

'(D) a country club membership;

'(E) a vacation or other noncampaign-related trip;

'(F) a household food item;

'(G) a tuition payment;

'(H) admission to a sporting event, concert, theater, or other form of entertainment not associated with an election campaign; and

'(I) dues, fees, and other payments to a health club or recreational facility.'.

SEC. 302. PROHIBITION OF FUNDRAISING ON FEDERAL PROPERTY.

Section 607 of title 18, United States Code, is amended--

(1) by striking subsection (a) and inserting the following:

'(a) PROHIBITION-

'(1) IN GENERAL- It shall be unlawful for any person to solicit or receive a donation of money or other thing of value in connection with a Federal, State, or local election from a person who is located in a room or building occupied in the discharge of official duties by an officer or employee of the United States. It shall be unlawful for an individual who is an officer or employee of the Federal Government, including the President, Vice President, and Members of Congress, to solicit or receive a donation of money or other thing of value in connection with a Federal, State, or local election, while in any room or building occupied in the discharge of official duties by an officer or employee of the United States, from any person.

'(2) PENALTY- A person who violates this section shall be fined not more than $5,000, imprisoned not more than 3 years, or both.'; and

-22-

(2) in subsection (b), by inserting `or Executive Office of the President' after `Congress'.

SEC. 303. STRENGTHENING FOREIGN MONEY BAN.

Section 319 of the Federal Election Campaign Act of 1971 (2 U.S.C. 441e) is amended--

(1) by striking the heading and inserting the following:
`CONTRIBUTIONS AND DONATIONS BY FOREIGN NATIONALS'; and

(2) by striking subsection (a) and inserting the following:

`(a) PROHIBITION- It shall be unlawful for--

`(1) a foreign national, directly or indirectly, to make--

`(A) a contribution or donation of money or other thing of value, or to make an express or implied promise to make a contribution or donation, in connection with a Federal, State, or local election;

`(B) a contribution or donation to a committee of a political party; or

`(C) an expenditure, independent expenditure, or disbursement for an electioneering communication (within the meaning of section 304(f)(3)); or

`(2) a person to solicit, accept, or receive a contribution or donation described in subparagraph (A) or (B) of paragraph (1) from a foreign national.'.

SEC. 304. MODIFICATION OF INDIVIDUAL CONTRIBUTION LIMITS IN RESPONSE TO EXPENDITURES FROM PERSONAL FUNDS.

(a) INCREASED LIMITS FOR INDIVIDUALS- Section 315 of the Federal Election Campaign Act of 1971 (2 U.S.C. 441a) is amended--

(1) in subsection (a)(1), by striking `No person' and inserting `Except as provided in subsection (i), no person'; and

(2) by adding at the end the following:

`(i) INCREASED LIMIT TO ALLOW RESPONSE TO EXPENDITURES FROM PERSONAL FUNDS-

`(1) INCREASE-

'(A) IN GENERAL- Subject to paragraph (2), if the opposition personal funds amount with respect to a candidate for election to the office of Senator exceeds the threshold amount, the limit under subsection (a)(1)(A) (in this subsection referred to as the 'applicable limit') with respect to that candidate shall be the increased limit.

'(B) THRESHOLD AMOUNT-

'(i) STATE-BY-STATE COMPETITIVE AND FAIR CAMPAIGN FORMULA- In this subsection, the threshold amount with respect to an election cycle of a candidate described in subparagraph (A) is an amount equal to the sum of--

'(I) $150,000; and

'(II) $0.04 multiplied by the voting age population.

'(ii) VOTING AGE POPULATION- In this subparagraph, the term 'voting age population' means in the case of a candidate for the office of Senator, the voting age population of the State of the candidate (as certified under section 315(e)).

'(C) INCREASED LIMIT- Except as provided in clause (ii), for purposes of subparagraph (A), if the opposition personal funds amount is over--

'(i) 2 times the threshold amount, but not over 4 times that amount--

'(I) the increased limit shall be 3 times the applicable limit; and

'(II) the limit under subsection (a)(3) shall not apply with respect to any contribution made with respect to a candidate if such contribution is made under the increased limit of subparagraph (A) during a period in which the candidate may accept such a contribution;

'(ii) 4 times the threshold amount, but not over 10 times that amount--

'(I) the increased limit shall be 6 times the applicable limit; and

-24-

'(II) the limit under subsection (a)(3) shall not apply with respect to any contribution made with respect to a candidate if such contribution is made under the increased limit of subparagraph (A) during a period in which the candidate may accept such a contribution; and

'(iii) 10 times the threshold amount--

'(I) the increased limit shall be 6 times the applicable limit;

'(II) the limit under subsection (a)(3) shall not apply with respect to any contribution made with respect to a candidate if such contribution is made under the increased limit of subparagraph (A) during a period in which the candidate may accept such a contribution; and

'(III) the limits under subsection (d) with respect to any expenditure by a State or national committee of a political party shall not apply.

'(D) OPPOSITION PERSONAL FUNDS AMOUNT- The opposition personal funds amount is an amount equal to the excess (if any) of--

'(i) the greatest aggregate amount of expenditures from personal funds (as defined in section 304(a)(6)(B)) that an opposing candidate in the same election makes; over

'(ii) the aggregate amount of expenditures from personal funds made by the candidate with respect to the election.

'(2) TIME TO ACCEPT CONTRIBUTIONS UNDER INCREASED LIMIT-

'(A) IN GENERAL- Subject to subparagraph (B), a candidate and the candidate's authorized committee shall not accept any contribution, and a party committee shall not make any expenditure, under the increased limit under paragraph (1)--

'(i) until the candidate has received notification of the opposition personal funds amount under section 304(a)(6)(B); and `(ii) to the extent that such contribution, when added to the aggregate amount of contributions previously accepted and party expenditures previously made under the increased limits under this subsection for the election cycle, exceeds 110 percent of the opposition personal funds amount.

`(B) EFFECT OF WITHDRAWAL OF AN OPPOSING CANDIDATE- A candidate and a candidate's authorized committee shall not accept any contribution and a party shall not make any expenditure under the increased limit after the date on which an opposing candidate ceases to be a candidate to the extent that the amount of such increased limit is attributable to such an opposing candidate.

`(3) DISPOSAL OF EXCESS CONTRIBUTIONS-

`(A) IN GENERAL- The aggregate amount of contributions accepted by a candidate or a candidate's authorized committee under the increased limit under paragraph (1) and not otherwise expended in connection with the election with respect to which such contributions relate shall, not later than 50 days after the date of such election, be used in the manner described in subparagraph (B).

`(B) RETURN TO CONTRIBUTORS- A candidate or a candidate's authorized committee shall return the excess contribution to the person who made the contribution.

`(j) LIMITATION ON REPAYMENT OF PERSONAL LOANS- Any candidate who incurs personal loans made after the effective date of the Bipartisan Campaign Reform Act of 2002 in connection with the candidate's campaign for election shall not repay (directly or indirectly), to the extent such loans exceed $250,000, such loans from any contributions made to such candidate or any authorized committee of such candidate after the date of such election.'.

(b) NOTIFICATION OF EXPENDITURES FROM PERSONAL FUNDS- Section 304(a)(6) of the Federal Election Campaign Act of 1971 (2 U.S.C. 434(a)(6)) is amended--

(1) by redesignating subparagraph (B) as subparagraph (E); and

(2) by inserting after subparagraph (A) the following:

`(B) NOTIFICATION OF EXPENDITURE FROM PERSONAL FUNDS-

`(i) DEFINITION OF EXPENDITURE FROM PERSONAL FUNDS- In this subparagraph, the term `expenditure from personal funds' means--

`(I) an expenditure made by a candidate using personal funds; and

`(II) a contribution or loan made by a candidate using personal funds or a loan secured using such funds to the candidate's authorized committee.

`(ii) DECLARATION OF INTENT- Not later than the date that is 15 days after the date on which an individual becomes a candidate for the office of Senator, the candidate shall file a declaration stating the total amount of expenditures from personal funds that the candidate intends to make, or to obligate to make, with respect to the election that will exceed the State-by-State competitive and fair campaign formula with--

`(I) the Commission; and

`(II) each candidate in the same election.

`(iii) INITIAL NOTIFICATION- Not later than 24 hours after a candidate described in clause (ii) makes or obligates to make an aggregate amount of expenditures from personal funds in excess of 2 times the threshold amount in connection with any election, the candidate shall file a notification with--

`(I) the Commission; and

`(II) each candidate in the same election.

`(iv) ADDITIONAL NOTIFICATION- After a candidate files an initial notification under clause (iii), the candidate shall file an additional notification each time expenditures from personal funds are made or obligated to be made in an aggregate amount that exceed $10,000 with--

`(I) the Commission; and

`(II) each candidate in the same election.

Such notification shall be filed not later than 24 hours after the expenditure is made.

`(v) CONTENTS- A notification under clause (iii) or (iv) shall include-

`(I) the name of the candidate and the office sought by the candidate;

`(II) the date and amount of each expenditure; and

-27-

'(III) the total amount of expenditures from personal funds that the candidate has made, or obligated to make, with respect to an election as of the date of the expenditure that is the subject of the notification.

'(C) NOTIFICATION OF DISPOSAL OF EXCESS CONTRIBUTIONS- In the next regularly scheduled report after the date of the election for which a candidate seeks nomination for election to, or election to, Federal office, the candidate or the candidate's authorized committee shall submit to the Commission a report indicating the source and amount of any excess contributions (as determined under paragraph (1) of section 315(i)) and the manner in which the candidate or the candidate's authorized committee used such funds.

'(D) ENFORCEMENT- For provisions providing for the enforcement of the reporting requirements under this paragraph, see section 309.'.

(c) DEFINITIONS- Section 301 of the Federal Election Campaign Act of 1971 (2 U.S.C. 431), as amended by section 101(b), is further amended by adding at the end the following:

'(25) ELECTION CYCLE- For purposes of sections 315(i) and 315A and paragraph (26), the term 'election cycle' means the period beginning on the day after the date of the most recent election for the specific office or seat that a candidate is seeking and ending on the date of the next election for that office or seat. For purposes of the preceding sentence, a primary election and a general election shall be considered to be separate elections.

'(26) PERSONAL FUNDS- The term 'personal funds' means an amount that is derived from--

'(A) any asset that, under applicable State law, at the time the individual became a candidate, the candidate had legal right of access to or control over, and with respect to which the candidate had--

'(i) legal and rightful title; or

'(ii) an equitable interest;

'(B) income received during the current election cycle of the candidate, including--

'(i) a salary and other earned income from bona fide employment;

'(ii) dividends and proceeds from the sale of the candidate's stocks or other investments;

-28-

`(iii) bequests to the candidate;

`(iv) income from trusts established before the beginning of the election cycle;

`(v) income from trusts established by bequest after the beginning of the election cycle of which the candidate is the beneficiary;

`(vi) gifts of a personal nature that had been customarily received by the candidate prior to the beginning of the election cycle; and

`(vii) proceeds from lotteries and similar legal games of chance; and

`(C) a portion of assets that are jointly owned by the candidate and the candidate's spouse equal to the candidate's share of the asset under the instrument of conveyance or ownership, but if no specific share is indicated by an instrument of conveyance or ownership, the value of 1/2 of the property.'.

SEC. 305. LIMITATION ON AVAILABILITY OF LOWEST UNIT CHARGE FOR FEDERAL CANDIDATES ATTACKING OPPOSITION.

(a) IN GENERAL- Section 315(b) of the Communications Act of 1934 (47 U.S.C. 315(b)) is amended--

(1) by striking `(b) The charges' and inserting the following:

`(b) CHARGES-

`(1) IN GENERAL- The charges';

(2) by redesignating paragraphs (1) and (2) as subparagraphs (A) and (B), respectively; and

(3) by adding at the end the following:

`(2) CONTENT OF BROADCASTS-

`(A) IN GENERAL- In the case of a candidate for Federal office, such candidate shall not be entitled to receive the rate under paragraph (1)(A) for the use of any broadcasting station unless the candidate provides written certification to the broadcast station that the candidate (and any authorized committee of the candidate) shall not make any direct reference to another candidate for the same office, in any broadcast using the rights and conditions of access under this Act,

-29-

unless such reference meets the requirements of subparagraph (C) or (D).

`(B) LIMITATION ON CHARGES- If a candidate for Federal office (or any authorized committee of such candidate) makes a reference described in subparagraph (A) in any broadcast that does not meet the requirements of subparagraph (C) or (D), such candidate shall not be entitled to receive the rate under paragraph (1)(A) for such broadcast or any other broadcast during any portion of the 45-day and 60-day periods described in paragraph (1)(A), that occur on or after the date of such broadcast, for election to such office.

`(C) TELEVISION BROADCASTS- A candidate meets the requirements of this subparagraph if, in the case of a television broadcast, at the end of such broadcast there appears simultaneously, for a period no less than 4 seconds--

`(i) a clearly identifiable photographic or similar image of the candidate; and

`(ii) a clearly readable printed statement, identifying the candidate and stating that the candidate has approved the broadcast and that the candidate's authorized committee paid for the broadcast.

`(D) RADIO BROADCASTS- A candidate meets the requirements of this subparagraph if, in the case of a radio broadcast, the broadcast includes a personal audio statement by the candidate that identifies the candidate, the office the candidate is seeking, and indicates that the candidate has approved the broadcast.

`(E) CERTIFICATION- Certifications under this section shall be provided and certified as accurate by the candidate (or any authorized committee of the candidate) at the time of purchase.

`(F) DEFINITIONS- For purposes of this paragraph, the terms `authorized committee' and `Federal office' have the meanings given such terms by section 301 of the Federal Election Campaign Act of 1971 (2 U.S.C. 431).'.

(b) CONFORMING AMENDMENT- Section 315(b)(1)(A) of the Communications Act of 1934 (47 U.S.C. 315(b)(1)(A)), as amended by this Act, is amended by inserting `subject to paragraph (2),' before `during the forty-five days'.

(c) EFFECTIVE DATE- The amendments made by this section shall apply to broadcasts made after the effective date of this Act.

SEC. 306. SOFTWARE FOR FILING REPORTS AND PROMPT DISCLOSURE OF CONTRIBUTIONS.

Section 304(a) of the Federal Election Campaign Act of 1971 (2 U.S.C. 434(a)) is amended by adding at the end the following:

'(12) SOFTWARE FOR FILING OF REPORTS-

'(A) IN GENERAL- The Commission shall--

'(i) promulgate standards to be used by vendors to develop software that--

'(I) permits candidates to easily record information concerning receipts and disbursements required to be reported under this Act at the time of the receipt or disbursement;

'(II) allows the information recorded under subclause (I) to be transmitted immediately to the Commission; and

'(III) allows the Commission to post the information on the Internet immediately upon receipt; and

'(ii) make a copy of software that meets the standards promulgated under clause (i) available to each person required to file a designation, statement, or report in electronic form under this Act.

'(B) ADDITIONAL INFORMATION- To the extent feasible, the Commission shall require vendors to include in the software developed under the standards under subparagraph (A) the ability for any person to file any designation, statement, or report required under this Act in electronic form.

'(C) REQUIRED USE- Notwithstanding any provision of this Act relating to times for filing reports, each candidate for Federal office (or that candidate's authorized committee) shall use software that meets the standards promulgated under this paragraph once such software is made available to such candidate.

'(D) REQUIRED POSTING- The Commission shall, as soon as practicable, post on the Internet any information received under this paragraph.'.

SEC. 307. MODIFICATION OF CONTRIBUTION LIMITS.

(a) INCREASE IN INDIVIDUAL LIMITS FOR CERTAIN CONTRIBUTIONS- Section 315(a)(1) of the Federal Election Campaign Act of 1971 (2 U.S.C. 441a(a)(1)) is amended--

(1) in subparagraph (A), by striking `$1,000' and inserting `$2,000'; and

(2) in subparagraph (B), by striking `$20,000' and inserting `$25,000'.

(b) INCREASE IN ANNUAL AGGREGATE LIMIT ON INDIVIDUAL CONTRIBUTIONS- Section 315(a)(3) of the Federal Election Campaign Act of 1971 (2 U.S.C. 441a(a)(3)) is amended to read as follows:

`(3) During the period which begins on January 1 of an odd-numbered year and ends on December 31 of the next even-numbered year, no individual may make contributions aggregating more than--

`(A) $37,500, in the case of contributions to candidates and the authorized committees of candidates;

`(B) $57,500, in the case of any other contributions, of which not more than $37,500 may be attributable to contributions to political committees which are not political committees of national political parties.'.

(c) INCREASE IN SENATORIAL CAMPAIGN COMMITTEE LIMIT- Section 315(h) of the Federal Election Campaign Act of 1971 (2 U.S.C. 441a(h)) is amended by striking `$17,500' and inserting `$35,000'.

(d) INDEXING OF CONTRIBUTION LIMITS- Section 315(c) of the Federal Election Campaign Act of 1971 (2 U.S.C. 441a(c)) is amended--

(1) in paragraph (1)--

(A) by striking the second and third sentences;

(B) by inserting `(A)' before `At the beginning'; and

(C) by adding at the end the following:

`(B) Except as provided in subparagraph (C), in any calendar year after 2002--

`(i) a limitation established by subsections (a)(1)(A), (a)(1)(B), (a)(3), (b), (d), or (h) shall be increased by the percent difference determined under subparagraph (A);

-32-

'(ii) each amount so increased shall remain in effect for the calendar year; and

'(iii) if any amount after adjustment under clause (i) is not a multiple of $100, such amount shall be rounded to the nearest multiple of $100.

'(C) In the case of limitations under subsections (a)(1)(A), (a)(1)(B), (a)(3), and (h), increases shall only be made in odd-numbered years and such increases shall remain in effect for the 2-year period beginning on the first day following the date of the last general election in the year preceding the year in which the amount is increased and ending on the date of the next general election.'; and

(2) in paragraph (2)(B), by striking 'means the calendar year 1974' and inserting 'means--

'(i) for purposes of subsections (b) and (d), calendar year 1974; and

'(ii) for purposes of subsections (a)(1)(A), (a)(1)(B), (a)(3), and (h), calendar year 2001'.

(e) EFFECTIVE DATE- The amendments made by this section shall apply with respect to contributions made on or after January 1, 2003.

SEC. 308. DONATIONS TO PRESIDENTIAL INAUGURAL COMMITTEE.

(a) IN GENERAL- Chapter 5 of title 36, United States Code, is amended by--

(1) redesignating section 510 as section 511; and

(2) inserting after section 509 the following:

'Sec. 510. Disclosure of and prohibition on certain donations

'(a) IN GENERAL- A committee shall not be considered to be the Inaugural Committee for purposes of this chapter unless the committee agrees to, and meets, the requirements of subsections (b) and (c).

'(b) DISCLOSURE-

'(1) IN GENERAL- Not later than the date that is 90 days after the date of the Presidential inaugural ceremony, the committee shall file a report with the Federal Election Commission disclosing any donation of money or anything of value made to the committee in an aggregate amount equal to or greater than $200.

'(2) CONTENTS OF REPORT- A report filed under paragraph (1) shall contain--

-33-

'(A) the amount of the donation;

'(B) the date the donation is received; and

'(C) the name and address of the person making the donation.

'(c) LIMITATION- The committee shall not accept any donation from a foreign national (as defined in section 319(b) of the Federal Election Campaign Act of 1971 (2 U.S.C. 441e(b))).'.

(b) REPORTS MADE AVAILABLE BY FEC- Section 304 of the Federal Election Campaign Act of 1971 (2 U.S.C. 434), as amended by sections 103, 201, and 212 is amended by adding at the end the following:

'(h) REPORTS FROM INAUGURAL COMMITTEES- The Federal Election Commission shall make any report filed by an Inaugural Committee under section 510 of title 36, United States Code, accessible to the public at the offices of the Commission and on the Internet not later than 48 hours after the report is received by the Commission.'.

SEC. 309. PROHIBITION ON FRAUDULENT SOLICITATION OF FUNDS.

Section 322 of the Federal Election Campaign Act of 1971 (2 U.S.C. 441h) is amended--

(1) by inserting '(a) IN GENERAL- ' before 'No person'; and

(2) by adding at the end the following:

'(b) FRAUDULENT SOLICITATION OF FUNDS- No person shall--

'(1) fraudulently misrepresent the person as speaking, writing, or otherwise acting for or on behalf of any candidate or political party or employee or agent thereof for the purpose of soliciting contributions or donations; or

'(2) willfully and knowingly participate in or conspire to participate in any plan, scheme, or design to violate paragraph (1).'.

SEC. 310. STUDY AND REPORT ON CLEAN MONEY CLEAN ELECTIONS LAWS.

(a) CLEAN MONEY CLEAN ELECTIONS DEFINED- In this section, the term 'clean money clean elections' means funds received under State laws that provide in whole or in part for the public financing of election campaigns.

(b) STUDY-

-34-

(1) IN GENERAL- The Comptroller General shall conduct a study of the clean money clean elections of Arizona and Maine.

(2) MATTERS STUDIED-

(A) STATISTICS ON CLEAN MONEY CLEAN ELECTIONS CANDIDATES- The Comptroller General shall determine--

(i) the number of candidates who have chosen to run for public office with clean money clean elections including--

(I) the office for which they were candidates;

(II) whether the candidate was an incumbent or a challenger; and

(III) whether the candidate was successful in the candidate's bid for public office; and

(ii) the number of races in which at least one candidate ran an election with clean money clean elections.

(B) EFFECTS OF CLEAN MONEY CLEAN ELECTIONS- The Comptroller General of the United States shall describe the effects of public financing under the clean money clean elections laws on the 2000 elections in Arizona and Maine.

(c) REPORT- Not later than 1 year after the date of enactment of this Act, the Comptroller General of the United States shall submit a report to the Congress detailing the results of the study conducted under subsection (b).

SEC. 311. CLARITY STANDARDS FOR IDENTIFICATION OF SPONSORS OF ELECTION-RELATED ADVERTISING.

Section 318 of the Federal Election Campaign Act of 1971 (2 U.S.C. 441d) is amended--

(1) in subsection (a)--

(A) in the matter preceding paragraph (1)--

(i) by striking `Whenever' and inserting `Whenever a political committee makes a disbursement for the purpose of financing any communication through any broadcasting station, newspaper, magazine, outdoor advertising facility, mailing, or any other type of general public political advertising, or whenever';

(ii) by striking `an expenditure' and inserting `a disbursement';

(iii) by striking `direct'; and

(iv) by inserting `or makes a disbursement for an electioneering communication (as defined in section 304(f)(3))' after `public political advertising'; and

(B) in paragraph (3), by inserting `and permanent street address, telephone number, or World Wide Web address' after `name'; and

(2) by adding at the end the following:

`(c) SPECIFICATION- Any printed communication described in subsection (a) shall--

`(1) be of sufficient type size to be clearly readable by the recipient of the communication;

`(2) be contained in a printed box set apart from the other contents of the communication; and

`(3) be printed with a reasonable degree of color contrast between the background and the printed statement.

`(d) ADDITIONAL REQUIREMENTS-

`(1) COMMUNICATIONS BY CANDIDATES OR AUTHORIZED PERSONS-

`(A) BY RADIO- Any communication described in paragraph (1) or (2) of subsection (a) which is transmitted through radio shall include, in addition to the requirements of that paragraph, an audio statement by the candidate that identifies the candidate and states that the candidate has approved the communication.

`(B) BY TELEVISION- Any communication described in paragraph (1) or (2) of subsection (a) which is transmitted through television shall include, in addition to the requirements of that paragraph, a statement that identifies the candidate and states that the candidate has approved the communication. Such statement--

`(i) shall be conveyed by--

    `(I) an unobscured, full-screen view of the candidate making the statement, or

    `(II) the candidate in voice-over, accompanied by a clearly identifiable photographic or similar image of the candidate; and

    `(ii) shall also appear in writing at the end of the communication in a clearly readable manner with a reasonable degree of color contrast between the background and the printed statement, for a period of at least 4 seconds.

`(2) COMMUNICATIONS BY OTHERS- Any communication described in paragraph (3) of subsection (a) which is transmitted through radio or television shall include, in addition to the requirements of that paragraph, in a clearly spoken manner, the following audio statement: `**XXXXX** is responsible for the content of this advertising.' (with the blank to be filled in with the name of the political committee or other person paying for the communication and the name of any connected organization of the payor). If transmitted through television, the statement shall be conveyed by an unobscured, full-screen view of a representative of the political committee or other person making the statement, or by a representative of such political committee or other person in voice-over, and shall also appear in a clearly readable manner with a reasonable degree of color contrast between the background and the printed statement, for a period of at least 4 seconds.'.

SEC. 312. INCREASE IN PENALTIES.

(a) IN GENERAL- Subparagraph (A) of section 309(d)(1) of the Federal Election Campaign Act of 1971 (2 U.S.C. 437g(d)(1)(A)) is amended to read as follows:

`(A) Any person who knowingly and willfully commits a violation of any provision of this Act which involves the making, receiving, or reporting of any contribution, donation, or expenditure--

    `(i) aggregating $25,000 or more during a calendar year shall be fined under title 18, United States Code, or imprisoned for not more than 5 years, or both; or

    `(ii) aggregating $2,000 or more (but less than $25,000) during a calendar year shall be fined under such title, or imprisoned for not more than 1 year, or both.'.

(b) EFFECTIVE DATE- The amendment made by this section shall apply to violations occurring on or after the effective date of this Act.

SEC. 313. STATUTE OF LIMITATIONS.

(a) IN GENERAL- Section 406(a) of the Federal Election Campaign Act of 1971 (2 U.S.C. 455(a)) is amended by striking `3' and inserting `5'.

(b) EFFECTIVE DATE- The amendment made by this section shall apply to violations occurring on or after the effective date of this Act.

SEC. 314. SENTENCING GUIDELINES.

(a) IN GENERAL- The United States Sentencing Commission shall--

(1) promulgate a guideline, or amend an existing guideline under section 994 of title 28, United States Code, in accordance with paragraph (2), for penalties for violations of the Federal Election Campaign Act of 1971 and related election laws; and

(2) submit to Congress an explanation of any guidelines promulgated under paragraph (1) and any legislative or administrative recommendations regarding enforcement of the Federal Election Campaign Act of 1971 and related election laws.

(b) CONSIDERATIONS- The Commission shall provide guidelines under subsection (a) taking into account the following considerations:

(1) Ensure that the sentencing guidelines and policy statements reflect the serious nature of such violations and the need for aggressive and appropriate law enforcement action to prevent such violations.

(2) Provide a sentencing enhancement for any person convicted of such violation if such violation involves--

(A) a contribution, donation, or expenditure from a foreign source;

(B) a large number of illegal transactions;

(C) a large aggregate amount of illegal contributions, donations, or expenditures;

(D) the receipt or disbursement of governmental funds; and

(E) an intent to achieve a benefit from the Federal Government.

(3) Assure reasonable consistency with other relevant directives and guidelines of the Commission.

(4) Account for aggravating or mitigating circumstances that might justify exceptions, including circumstances for which the sentencing guidelines currently provide sentencing enhancements.

(5) Assure the guidelines adequately meet the purposes of sentencing under section 3553(a)(2) of title 18, United States Code.

(c) EFFECTIVE DATE; EMERGENCY AUTHORITY TO PROMULGATE GUIDELINES-

(1) EFFECTIVE DATE- Notwithstanding section 402, the United States Sentencing Commission shall promulgate guidelines under this section not later than the later of--

(A) 90 days after the effective date of this Act; or

(B) 90 days after the date on which at least a majority of the members of the Commission are appointed and holding office.

(2) EMERGENCY AUTHORITY TO PROMULGATE GUIDELINES- The Commission shall promulgate guidelines under this section in accordance with the procedures set forth in section 21(a) of the Sentencing Reform Act of 1987, as though the authority under such Act has not expired.

SEC. 315. INCREASE IN PENALTIES IMPOSED FOR VIOLATIONS OF CONDUIT CONTRIBUTION BAN.

(a) INCREASE IN CIVIL MONEY PENALTY FOR KNOWING AND WILLFUL VIOLATIONS- Section 309(a) of the Federal Election Campaign Act of 1971 (2 U.S.C. 437g(a)) is amended--

(1) in paragraph (5)(B), by inserting before the period at the end the following: `(or, in the case of a violation of section 320, which is not less than 300 percent of the amount involved in the violation and is not more than the greater of $50,000 or 1,000 percent of the amount involved in the violation)'; and

(2) in paragraph (6)(C), by inserting before the period at the end the following: `(or, in the case of a violation of section 320, which is not less than 300 percent of the amount involved in the violation and is not more than the greater of $50,000 or 1,000 percent of the amount involved in the violation)'.

(b) INCREASE IN CRIMINAL PENALTY- Section 309(d)(1) of such Act (2 U.S.C. 437g(d)(1)) is amended by adding at the end the following new subparagraph:

`(D) Any person who knowingly and willfully commits a violation of section 320 involving an amount aggregating more than $10,000 during a calendar year shall be--

`(i) imprisoned for not more than 2 years if the amount is less than $25,000 (and subject to imprisonment under subparagraph (A) if the amount is $25,000 or more);

`(ii) fined not less than 300 percent of the amount involved in the violation and not more than the greater of--

`(I) $50,000; or

`(II) 1,000 percent of the amount involved in the violation; or

`(iii) both imprisoned under clause (i) and fined under clause (ii).'.

(c) EFFECTIVE DATE- The amendments made by this section shall apply with respect to violations occurring on or after the effective date of this Act.

SEC. 316. RESTRICTION ON INCREASED CONTRIBUTION LIMITS BY TAKING INTO ACCOUNT CANDIDATE'S AVAILABLE FUNDS.

Section 315(i)(1) of the Federal Election Campaign Act of 1971 (2 U.S.C. 441a(i)(1)), as added by this Act, is amended by adding at the end the following:

`(E) SPECIAL RULE FOR CANDIDATE'S CAMPAIGN FUNDS-

`(i) IN GENERAL- For purposes of determining the aggregate amount of expenditures from personal funds under subparagraph (D)(ii), such amount shall include the gross receipts advantage of the candidate's authorized committee.

`(ii) GROSS RECEIPTS ADVANTAGE- For purposes of clause (i), the term `gross receipts advantage' means the excess, if any, of--

`(I) the aggregate amount of 50 percent of gross receipts of a candidate's authorized committee during any election cycle (not including contributions from personal funds of the candidate) that may be expended in connection with the election, as determined on June 30 and December 31 of the year preceding the year in which a general election is held, over

`(II) the aggregate amount of 50 percent of gross receipts of the opposing candidate's authorized committee during any election cycle (not including contributions from personal funds of the candidate) that may be expended in connection with the election, as determined on June 30 and December 31 of the year preceding the year in which a general election is held.'.

SEC. 317. CLARIFICATION OF RIGHT OF NATIONALS OF THE UNITED STATES TO MAKE POLITICAL CONTRIBUTIONS.

Section 319(b)(2) of the Federal Election Campaign Act of 1971 (2 U.S.C. 441e(b)(2)) is amended by inserting after `United States' the following: `or a national of the United States (as defined in section 101(a)(22) of the Immigration and Nationality Act)'.

SEC. 318. PROHIBITION OF CONTRIBUTIONS BY MINORS.

Title III of the Federal Election Campaign Act of 1971 (2 U.S.C. 431 et seq.), as amended by section 101, is further amended by adding at the end the following new section:

`PROHIBITION OF CONTRIBUTIONS BY MINORS

`SEC. 324. An individual who is 17 years old or younger shall not make a contribution to a candidate or a contribution or donation to a committee of a political party.'.

SEC. 319. MODIFICATION OF INDIVIDUAL CONTRIBUTION LIMITS FOR HOUSE CANDIDATES IN RESPONSE TO EXPENDITURES FROM PERSONAL FUNDS.

(a) INCREASED LIMITS- Title III of the Federal Election Campaign Act of 1971 (2 U.S.C. 431 et seq.) is amended by inserting after section 315 the following new section:

`MODIFICATION OF CERTAIN LIMITS FOR HOUSE CANDIDATES IN RESPONSE TO PERSONAL FUND EXPENDITURES OF OPPONENTS

`SEC. 315A. (a) AVAILABILITY OF INCREASED LIMIT-

`(1) IN GENERAL- Subject to paragraph (3), if the opposition personal funds amount with respect to a candidate for election to the office of Representative in, or Delegate or Resident Commissioner to, the Congress exceeds $350,000--

`(A) the limit under subsection (a)(1)(A) with respect to the candidate shall be tripled;

'(B) the limit under subsection (a)(3) shall not apply with respect to any contribution made with respect to the candidate if the contribution is made under the increased limit allowed under subparagraph (A) during a period in which the candidate may accept such a contribution; and

'(C) the limits under subsection (d) with respect to any expenditure by a State or national committee of a political party on behalf of the candidate shall not apply.

'(2) DETERMINATION OF OPPOSITION PERSONAL FUNDS AMOUNT-

'(A) IN GENERAL- The opposition personal funds amount is an amount equal to the excess (if any) of--

'(i) the greatest aggregate amount of expenditures from personal funds (as defined in subsection (b)(1)) that an opposing candidate in the same election makes; over

'(ii) the aggregate amount of expenditures from personal funds made by the candidate with respect to the election.

'(B) SPECIAL RULE FOR CANDIDATE'S CAMPAIGN FUNDS-

'(i) IN GENERAL- For purposes of determining the aggregate amount of expenditures from personal funds under subparagraph (A), such amount shall include the gross receipts advantage of the candidate's authorized committee.

'(ii) GROSS RECEIPTS ADVANTAGE- For purposes of clause (i), the term 'gross receipts advantage' means the excess, if any, of--

'(I) the aggregate amount of 50 percent of gross receipts of a candidate's authorized committee during any election cycle (not including contributions from personal funds of the candidate) that may be expended in connection with the election, as determined on June 30 and December 31 of the year preceding the year in which a general election is held, over

'(II) the aggregate amount of 50 percent of gross receipts of the opposing candidate's authorized committee during any election cycle (not including contributions from personal funds of the candidate) that may be expended in connection with the election, as determined on June 30 and December 31 of the year preceding the year in which a general election is held.

`(3) TIME TO ACCEPT CONTRIBUTIONS UNDER INCREASED LIMIT-

`(A) IN GENERAL- Subject to subparagraph (B), a candidate and the candidate's authorized committee shall not accept any contribution, and a party committee shall not make any expenditure, under the increased limit under paragraph (1)--

`(i) until the candidate has received notification of the opposition personal funds amount under subsection (b)(1); and

`(ii) to the extent that such contribution, when added to the aggregate amount of contributions previously accepted and party expenditures previously made under the increased limits under this subsection for the election cycle, exceeds 100 percent of the opposition personal funds amount.

`(B) EFFECT OF WITHDRAWAL OF AN OPPOSING CANDIDATE- A candidate and a candidate's authorized committee shall not accept any contribution and a party shall not make any expenditure under the increased limit after the date on which an opposing candidate ceases to be a candidate to the extent that the amount of such increased limit is attributable to such an opposing candidate.

`(4) DISPOSAL OF EXCESS CONTRIBUTIONS-

`(A) IN GENERAL- The aggregate amount of contributions accepted by a candidate or a candidate's authorized committee under the increased limit under paragraph (1) and not otherwise expended in connection with the election with respect to which such contributions relate shall, not later than 50 days after the date of such election, be used in the manner described in subparagraph (B).

`(B) RETURN TO CONTRIBUTORS- A candidate or a candidate's authorized committee shall return the excess contribution to the person who made the contribution.

`(b) NOTIFICATION OF EXPENDITURES FROM PERSONAL FUNDS-

'(1) IN GENERAL-

'(A) DEFINITION OF EXPENDITURE FROM PERSONAL FUNDS- In this paragraph, the term 'expenditure from personal funds' means--

'(i) an expenditure made by a candidate using personal funds; and

'(ii) a contribution or loan made by a candidate using personal funds or a loan secured using such funds to the candidate's authorized committee.

'(B) DECLARATION OF INTENT- Not later than the date that is 15 days after the date on which an individual becomes a candidate for the office of Representative in, or Delegate or Resident Commissioner to, the Congress, the candidate shall file a declaration stating the total amount of expenditures from personal funds that the candidate intends to make, or to obligate to make, with respect to the election that will exceed $350,000.

'(C) INITIAL NOTIFICATION- Not later than 24 hours after a candidate described in subparagraph (B) makes or obligates to make an aggregate amount of expenditures from personal funds in excess of $350,000 in connection with any election, the candidate shall file a notification.

'(D) ADDITIONAL NOTIFICATION- After a candidate files an initial notification under subparagraph (C), the candidate shall file an additional notification each time expenditures from personal funds are made or obligated to be made in an aggregate amount that exceeds $10,000. Such notification shall be filed not later than 24 hours after the expenditure is made.

'(E) CONTENTS- A notification under subparagraph (C) or (D) shall include--

'(i) the name of the candidate and the office sought by the candidate;

'(ii) the date and amount of each expenditure; and

'(iii) the total amount of expenditures from personal funds that the candidate has made, or obligated to make, with respect to an election as of the date of the expenditure that is the subject of the notification.

'(F) PLACE OF FILING- Each declaration or notification required to be filed by a candidate under subparagraph (C), (D), or (E) shall be filed with--

'(i) the Commission; and

'(ii) each candidate in the same election and the national party of each such candidate.

'(2) NOTIFICATION OF DISPOSAL OF EXCESS CONTRIBUTIONS- In the next regularly scheduled report after the date of the election for which a candidate seeks nomination for election to, or election to, Federal office, the candidate or the candidate's authorized committee shall submit to the Commission a report indicating the source and amount of any excess contributions (as determined under subsection (a)) and the manner in which the candidate or the candidate's authorized committee used such funds.

'(3) ENFORCEMENT- For provisions providing for the enforcement of the reporting requirements under this subsection, see section 309.'.

(b) CONFORMING AMENDMENT- Section 315(a)(1) of the Federal Election Campaign Act of 1971 (2 U.S.C. 441a), as amended by section 304(a), is amended by striking `subsection (i),' and inserting `subsection (i) and section 315A,'.

TITLE IV--SEVERABILITY; EFFECTIVE DATE

SEC. 401. SEVERABILITY.

If any provision of this Act or amendment made by this Act, or the application of a provision or amendment to any person or circumstance, is held to be unconstitutional, the remainder of this Act and amendments made by this Act, and the application of the provisions and amendment to any person or circumstance, shall not be affected by the holding.

SEC. 402. EFFECTIVE DATES AND REGULATIONS.

(a) GENERAL EFFECTIVE DATE-

(1) IN GENERAL- Except as provided in the succeeding provisions of this section, the effective date of this Act, and the amendments made by this Act, is November 6, 2002.

(2) MODIFICATION OF CONTRIBUTION LIMITS- The amendments made by--

(A) section 102 shall apply with respect to contributions made on or after January 1, 2003; and

(B) section 307 shall take effect as provided in subsection (e) of such section.

(3) SEVERABILITY; EFFECTIVE DATES AND REGULATIONS; JUDICIAL REVIEW- Title IV shall take effect on the date of enactment of this Act.

(4) PROVISIONS NOT TO APPLY TO RUNOFF ELECTIONS- Section 323(b) of the Federal Election Campaign Act of 1971 (as added by section 101(a)), section 103(a), title II, sections 304 (including section 315(j) of Federal Election Campaign Act of 1971, as added by section 304(a)(2)), 305 (notwithstanding subsection (c) of such section), 311, 316, 318, and 319, and title V (and the amendments made by such sections and titles) shall take effect on November 6, 2002, but shall not apply with respect to runoff elections, recounts, or election contests resulting from elections held prior to such date.

(b) SOFT MONEY OF NATIONAL POLITICAL PARTIES-

(1) IN GENERAL- Except for subsection (b) of such section, section 323 of the Federal Election Campaign Act of 1971 (as added by section 101(a)) shall take effect on November 6, 2002.

(2) TRANSITIONAL RULES FOR THE SPENDING OF SOFT MONEY OF NATIONAL POLITICAL PARTIES-

(A) IN GENERAL- Notwithstanding section 323(a) of the Federal Election Campaign Act of 1971 (as added by section 101(a)), if a national committee of a political party described in such section (including any person who is subject to such section under paragraph (2) of such section), has received funds described in such section prior to November 6, 2002, the rules described in subparagraph (B) shall apply with respect to the spending of the amount of such funds in the possession of such committee as of such date.

(B) USE OF EXCESS SOFT MONEY FUNDS-

(i) IN GENERAL- Subject to clauses (ii) and (iii), the national committee of a political party may use the amount described in subparagraph (A) prior to January 1, 2003, solely for the purpose of--

(I) retiring outstanding debts or obligations that were incurred solely in connection with an election held prior to November 6, 2002; or

(II) paying expenses or retiring outstanding debts or paying for obligations that were incurred solely in connection with any runoff election, recount, or election contest resulting from an election held prior to November 6, 2002.

(ii) PROHIBITION ON USING SOFT MONEY FOR HARD MONEY EXPENSES, DEBTS, AND OBLIGATIONS- A national committee of a political party may not use the amount described in subparagraph (A) for any expenditure (as defined in section 301(9) of the Federal Election Campaign Act of 1971 (2 U.S.C. 431(9))) or for retiring outstanding debts or obligations that were incurred for such an expenditure.

(iii) PROHIBITION OF BUILDING FUND USES- A national committee of a political party may not use the amount described in subparagraph (A) for activities to defray the costs of the construction or purchase of any office building or facility.

(c) REGULATIONS-

(1) IN GENERAL- Except as provided in paragraph (2), the Federal Election Commission shall promulgate regulations to carry out this Act and the amendments made by this Act that are under the Commission's jurisdiction not later than 270 days after the date of enactment of this Act.

(2) SOFT MONEY OF POLITICAL PARTIES- Not later than 90 days after the date of enactment of this Act, the Federal Election Commission shall promulgate regulations to carry out title I of this Act and the amendments made by such title.

SEC. 403. JUDICIAL REVIEW.

(a) SPECIAL RULES FOR ACTIONS BROUGHT ON CONSTITUTIONAL GROUNDS- If any action is brought for declaratory or injunctive relief to challenge the constitutionality of any provision of this Act or any amendment made by this Act, the following rules shall apply:

(1) The action shall be filed in the United States District Court for the District of Columbia and shall be heard by a 3-judge court convened pursuant to section 2284 of title 28, United States Code.

(2) A copy of the complaint shall be delivered promptly to the Clerk of the House of Representatives and the Secretary of the Senate.

(3) A final decision in the action shall be reviewable only by appeal directly to the Supreme Court of the United States. Such appeal shall be taken by the filing of a notice of appeal within 10 days, and the filing of a jurisdictional statement within 30 days, of the entry of the final decision.

(4) It shall be the duty of the United States District Court for the District of Columbia and the Supreme Court of the United States to advance on the docket and to expedite to the greatest possible extent the disposition of the action and appeal.

(b) INTERVENTION BY MEMBERS OF CONGRESS- In any action in which the constitutionality of any provision of this Act or any amendment made by this Act is raised (including but not limited to an action described in subsection (a)), any member of the House of Representatives (including a Delegate or Resident Commissioner to the Congress) or Senate shall have the right to intervene either in support of or opposition to the position of a party to the case regarding the constitutionality of the provision or amendment. To avoid duplication of efforts and reduce the burdens placed on the parties to the action, the court in any such action may make such orders as it considers necessary, including orders to require intervenors taking similar positions to file joint papers or to be represented by a single attorney at oral argument.

(c) CHALLENGE BY MEMBERS OF CONGRESS- Any Member of Congress may bring an action, subject to the special rules described in subsection (a), for declaratory or injunctive relief to challenge the constitutionality of any provision of this Act or any amendment made by this Act.

(d) APPLICABILITY-

(1) INITIAL CLAIMS- With respect to any action initially filed on or before December 31, 2006, the provisions of subsection (a) shall apply with respect to each action described in such section.

(2) SUBSEQUENT ACTIONS- With respect to any action initially filed after December 31, 2006, the provisions of subsection (a) shall not apply to any action described in such section unless the person filing such action elects such provisions to apply to the action.

TITLE V--ADDITIONAL DISCLOSURE PROVISIONS

SEC. 501. INTERNET ACCESS TO RECORDS.

Section 304(a)(11)(B) of the Federal Election Campaign Act of 1971 (2 U.S.C. 434(a)(11)(B)) is amended to read as follows:

`(B) The Commission shall make a designation, statement, report, or notification that is filed with the Commission under this Act available for inspection by the public in the offices of the Commission and accessible to the public on the Internet not later than 48 hours (or not later than 24 hours in the case of a designation, statement, report, or notification filed electronically) after receipt by the Commission.'.

SEC. 502. MAINTENANCE OF WEBSITE OF ELECTION REPORTS.

(a) IN GENERAL- The Federal Election Commission shall maintain a central site on the Internet to make accessible to the public all publicly available election-related reports and information.

(b) ELECTION-RELATED REPORT- In this section, the term 'election-related report' means any report, designation, or statement required to be filed under the Federal Election Campaign Act of 1971.

(c) COORDINATION WITH OTHER AGENCIES- Any Federal executive agency receiving election-related information which that agency is required by law to publicly disclose shall cooperate and coordinate with the Federal Election Commission to make such report available through, or for posting on, the site of the Federal Election Commission in a timely manner.

SEC. 503. ADDITIONAL DISCLOSURE REPORTS.

(a) PRINCIPAL CAMPAIGN COMMITTEES- Section 304(a)(2)(B) of the Federal Election Campaign Act of 1971 is amended by striking 'the following reports' and all that follows through the period and inserting 'the treasurer shall file quarterly reports, which shall be filed not later than the 15th day after the last day of each calendar quarter, and which shall be complete as of the last day of each calendar quarter, except that the report for the quarter ending December 31 shall be filed not later than January 31 of the following calendar year.'.

(b) NATIONAL COMMITTEE OF A POLITICAL PARTY- Section 304(a)(4) of such Act (2 U.S.C. 434(a)(4)) is amended by adding at the end the following flush sentence: 'Notwithstanding the preceding sentence, a national committee of a political party shall file the reports required under subparagraph (B).'.

SEC. 504. PUBLIC ACCESS TO BROADCASTING RECORDS.

Section 315 of the Communications Act of 1934 (47 U.S.C. 315), as amended by this Act, is amended by redesignating subsections (e) and (f) as subsections (f) and (g), respectively, and inserting after subsection (d) the following:

'(e) POLITICAL RECORD-

'(1) IN GENERAL- A licensee shall maintain, and make available for public inspection, a complete record of a request to purchase broadcast time that--

'(A) is made by or on behalf of a legally qualified candidate for public office; or

'(B) communicates a message relating to any political matter of national importance, including--

'(i) a legally qualified candidate;

'(ii) any election to Federal office; or

'(iii) a national legislative issue of public importance.

'(2) CONTENTS OF RECORD- A record maintained under paragraph (1) shall contain information regarding--

'(A) whether the request to purchase broadcast time is accepted or rejected by the licensee;

'(B) the rate charged for the broadcast time;

'(C) the date and time on which the communication is aired;

'(D) the class of time that is purchased;

'(E) the name of the candidate to which the communication refers and the office to which the candidate is seeking election, the election to which the communication refers, or the issue to which the communication refers (as applicable);

'(F) in the case of a request made by, or on behalf of, a candidate, the name of the candidate, the authorized committee of the candidate, and the treasurer of such committee; and

'(G) in the case of any other request, the name of the person purchasing the time, the name, address, and phone number of a contact person for such person, and a list of the chief executive officers or members of the executive committee or of the board of directors of such person.

'(3) TIME TO MAINTAIN FILE- The information required under this subsection shall be placed in a political file as soon as possible and shall be retained by the licensee for a period of not less than 2 years.'.

Speaker of the House of Representatives.

Vice President of the United States and President of the Senate.

END

Statement by the President On Signing
the "Bipartisan Campaign Reform Act of 2002"

Today I have signed into law H.R. 2356, the "Bipartisan Campaign Reform Act of 2002." I believe that this legislation, although far from perfect, will improve the current financing system for Federal campaigns.

The bill reforms our system of financing campaigns in several important ways. First, it will prevent unions and corporations from making unregulated, "soft" money contributions -- a legislative step for which I repeatedly have called. Often, these groups take political action without the consent of their members or shareholders, so that the influence of these groups on elections does not necessarily comport with the actual views of the individuals who comprise these organizations. This prohibition will help to right that imbalance. Second, this law will raise the decades-old limits on giving imposed on individuals who wish to support the candidate of their choice, thereby advancing my stated principle that election reform should strengthen the role of individual citizens in the political process. Third, this legislation creates new disclosure requirements and compels speedier compliance with existing ones, which will promote the free and swift flow of information to the public regarding the activities of groups and individuals in the political process. I long have believed that complete and immediate disclosure of the source of campaign contributions is the best way to reform campaign finance.

These provisions of the bill will go a long way toward fixing some of the most pressing problems in campaign finance today. They will result in an election finance system that encourages greater individual participation, and provides the public more accurate and timely information, than does the present system. All of the American electorate will benefit from these measures to strengthen our democracy.

However, the bill does have flaws. Certain provisions present serious constitutional concerns. In particular, H.R. 2356 goes farther than I originally proposed by preventing all individuals, not just unions and corporations, from making donations to political parties in connection with Federal elections. I believe individual freedom to participate in elections should be expanded, not diminished; and when individual freedoms are restricted, questions arise under the First Amendment. I also have reservations about the constitutionality of the broad ban on issue advertising, which restrains the speech of a wide variety of groups on issues of public import in the months closest to an election. I expect that the courts will resolve these legitimate legal questions as appropriate under the law.

As a policy matter, I would have preferred a bill that included a provision to protect union members and shareholders from involuntary political activities undertaken by their leadership. Individuals have a right not to have their money spent in support of candidates or causes with which they disagree, and those rights should be better protected by law. I hope that in the future the Congress and I can work together to remedy this defect of the current financing structure.

This legislation is the culmination of more than 6 years of debate among a vast array of legislators, citizens, and groups. Accordingly, it does not represent the full ideals of any one point of view. But it does represent progress in this often-contentious area of public policy debate. Taken as a whole, this bill improves the current system of financing for Federal campaigns, and therefore I have signed it into law.

GEORGE W. BUSH
THE WHITE HOUSE,
March 27, 2002.